MAGIC *and*
WITCHCRAFT
in SCOTLAND

MAGIC *and* WITCHCRAFT *in* SCOTLAND

JOYCE MILLER

GOBLINSHEAD
Musselburgh

Magic and Witchcraft in Scotland

First Published 2004
Reprinted 2005, 2010 (with some updating)
© Joyce Miller 2004, 2010

Published by GOBLINSHEAD
130B Inveresk Road
Musselburgh EH21 7AY Scotland

British Library Cataloguing in Publication Data
A catalogue record for this book is available from the British Library.

ISBN 1 899874 46 1/978 1899874 46 0

Printed by Bell & Bain, Glasgow
Typeset by GOBLINSHEAD

If you would like a full colour leaflet of our books on Scottish history, travel, castles and the supernatural, please contact us at:
Goblinshead, 130B Inveresk Road
Musselburgh EH21 7AY, Scotland
Tel: **0131 665 2894**
Email: **goblinshead@sol.co.uk**

Written, printed and published in Scotland

Contents

ACKNOWLEDGEMENTS

I would like to thank a number of people for their help with this book. Special thanks go to Martin at Goblinshead for his continued help and encouragement to get the book finished.

Most of the photographs are by Martin Coventry and Joyce Miller. I would also like to thank Helen Nicoll at the National Museums of Scotland, Lizanne Henderson, Martin Rackwitz, Tina Gibson and Bob Watts at City Litho for their help.

Illustrations are reproduced by kind permission of:

- **The Trustees of the National Museums of Scotland** for the silver heart brooch, the elfshot and molluka bean amulets and the lammer (amber) beads.

- **Padeapix** for photos of the Clootie Tree on the Doon Hill and Aberfoyle Kirkyard with Doon Hill.

- **Martin Rackwitz** for the photo of the Maggie Walls monument in Dunning.

- **Tina Gibson** for photographs of St Queran's Well at Islesteps.

LIST OF ILLUSTRATIONS

Illustrations are between pages 74 and 75.

Preface

This book is an introduction to the complicated subject of magic and witchcraft belief in early-modern Scotland. It is the result of many years' research in, and teaching of, the period between the sixteenth and eighteenth centuries when women, men and some children were accused of witchcraft. As with any subject, students and interested people want simple explanations for what happened during these years, but this is very difficult because witchcraft, and particularly its prosecution, is an emotive topic. This is partly because of the violent nature of the accusations and the investigations. It is also because individuals were executed as a result. Students often have difficulty with the subject because much of the material that is published and written relates to the prosecution of people accused of witchcraft. They find it difficult to accept the fact that those investigating accusations appear to have believed what was said in the confessions or that those who confessed might have been describing something that was true. They cannot understand why society appears to have been so credulous about something that to us is patently impossible and untrue. But then, what is truth? Is it possible for us to make judgements about what was true and what was fabricated without understanding something of the mind-set and culture of the time?

In order to understand the significance of witchcraft as a whole to early-modern society, and not just its prosecution, some discussion of the wider topic of magic is necessary. This provides the cultural background and context for witchcraft; it was not an anomalous or whimsical belief system. It was firmly grounded in the culture of the period and was recognised, and used, by both educated and non-literate people alike. Attitudes did change towards magic and, for some, it was seen as not only erroneous, but heretical. This critical and suspicious position provided the impetus for the criminalisation of the practice by both church and legal authorities.

The second part of the book is about witchcraft: its practice and prosecution. Explanation is given about intellectual demonological ideas and how witchcraft was seen to be harmful. The prosecution of individuals often appears to be given too much attention but this is because much of the evidence that survives relates to investigations and trials. To some extent this is also confirmed by the selection of places of interest that are connected with witches or witchcraft: many of them have negative or violent associations because they are the sites of executions or imprisonment. Some of them may have been the sites where groups of people met to conduct their demonic practices. This is the nature of the evidence rather than any personal choice on my part. But this book is not only about witchcraft; it is also about magic. There are more places of interest associated with magic and healing or beneficial witchcraft, which may indicate that magic had a much more significant role to play in early-modern society and beyond than witchcraft on its own.

The book will appeal to anyone with an interest in the subject, both visitors and locals. The sites mentioned as places of interest are included to provide geographical and historical location in order to give some context of time and place. The map gives approximate locations for the sites listed.

Although many of the sites are open to the public, others are on private land and should not be visited without permission. Some of them may also be in difficult and inaccessible locations, or they may be in a ruinous condition. Care should be taken when visiting unmanned sites. Further reading and an index are also provided.

Joyce Miller
Musselburgh
May 2004

How to Use the Book

There are three sections in this book.

The first section includes a general introduction and discussion of magic and its uses. This covers the historical background and changes in ideas about magic.

The second section covers more specifically demonic magic or witchcraft. It discusses attitudes towards witchcraft and how it was perceived as a crime. It also covers the accusations and investigations of witchcraft that took place in Scotland between 1563 and 1736.

The third section of the book covers places of interest that can be visited or seen. This section also includes a map. The places of interest section includes more detailed information on sites that are mentioned in the text and, where available, information on access and opening is given. This section also includes some sites that are not specifically mentioned but have some connection with the general themes of the book. The entries consist of a name; location; national grid reference (where known); description of site, and history. Facilities, opening and contact details are listed where available. It should be assumed that manned visitor attractions will be closed at Christmas and New Year unless otherwise stated.

While information has been checked it is recommended that anyone intending to visit should confirm details locally. Some sites are on private land and should not be visited without permission of the landowner.

A list of further reading follows the places of interest, then an index.

INTRODUCTION

What is meant by magic? People have always been quick to focus on the sensational aspects of magic, including the prosecution of suspected witches between the sixteenth and eighteenth centuries. Witchcraft is only one type of magic, but it illustrates that all levels of society understood the concept of a magical universe or world. This book will examine these ideas, and also consider the practical context of magical belief and practice.

How did early-modern society perceive the world, and what did they mean by a magical universe? Before the advent of rational science – even before the introduction of Christianity – society regarded the world not just in terms of the physical realm but incorporated a spiritual one as well, one which we might regard as being a form of magical realm. These different realms provided the basis for understanding the world and creation. Indeed, magic and the spiritual realm provided much of the foundation around which religious belief systems were developed. God – or Gods for some societies – existed amongst a celestial entourage of beings.

In the Christian world there were angels, archangels and others who inhabited heaven. God's counterpart, The Devil, commanded a rival band of demons and inhabited hell or the underworld. The powers and movements of the planets and stars also influenced earthly life events and outcomes. The concepts of heaven and hell, as well as purgatory, were well understood by medieval society: the term 'middle-erd' referred to our world, viewed as being half way between heaven and hell. For some, middle-earth may even have represented a place of purgatory, or limbo, where they existed prior to their ultimate destination.

Even on earth, or middle-earth, other powers were recognised, specifically those of nature. Water, rivers, fire, air, earth, stone and even trees had special powers or attendant spirits. These spirits, including fairies and ghosts, existed in other realms, as well as potentially in middle-earth. These worlds or realms did not necessarily exist in the same temporal or spatial plane as ours. It was acknowledged, however, that other-world realms could interface at liminal places, such as streams, wells, rivers, boundaries, bridges and hillsides, or times, such as midnight, sunrise or calendar festival days (Hallowe'en being the best known in present times), where the boundaries overlapped or touched.

Although not everyone engaged actively with all of these supernatural or preternatural powers, most of society participated to a greater or lesser degree, in both sacred and profane ways, by attempting to manipulate the occult powers of nature. Few tried to discover the secret of turning base metals to gold – otherwise known as alchemy – or to invoke the powers of spirits to cause serious harm through sorcery and witchcraft. Most people utilised magic on a much smaller scale, usually on a very personal level as a means to ensure a good crop or to identify future life partners.

Participating in magical beliefs and practices did, of course, lead to problems, as the church interpreted these beliefs as blasphemous, sacrilegious and heretical. Some students of magic, particularly those alchemists who attempted to reveal the secret of life, saw it as a noble pursuit and defended their practices. They argued that they were attempting to understand the secrets of everything in nature as part of God's creation, and saw their work as a virtuous philosophical endeavour. Not surprisingly, their opponents claimed that any attempt to invoke any power that was not God's was both dangerous and evil.

Although there were marked distinctions between the official doctrine and ritual of the church and the unofficial ritual of magic, there was a degree of overlap, especially before the Reformation. Pre-Reformation church ritual was often used to procure personal protection and help, particularly fertility and recovery from illness, both of which were also important outcomes of magical practice. On the other hand, some magical rites incorporated elements or objects of Christian formulae. The distinction between the two may not always have been clear for some people.

Different categories of magic were practised and most required a degree of instruction and expertise. The basic classifications of magic were ceremonial, natural, sorcery or artificial, and demonic. Ceremonial magic involved rituals that were intended to raise the spiritual understanding of the individual. Natural magic manipulated the naturally occurring occult forces of nature to create effects and was seen as a form of science. Artificial magic or sorcery used props and conjuring to effect outcomes. Demonic magic involved the invocation of demonic or evil spirits to create the desired outcome and was regarded as a perversion of religion. For some authorities, demonic magic was the same as witchcraft because it was assumed that demonic magic would be used for harmful purposes. It was the perception of intended harmful outcome that identified witchcraft as a form of demonic magic in earlier centuries.

There were other forms of magic, however, that were not perceived as particularly specialised. These included rituals and signs, often associated with special times of year, that were observed collectively by communities which were not regarded as specifically magical. Signs of any kind were important because certain events could be regarded as indicators predicting good or bad luck. Of equal importance, however, were rituals: repeated actions following a set pattern that were deemed to be significant. The survival of a community was paramount and people were willing to use any, and all, means to ensure this; and this often meant observing particular ceremonies or rituals. Cultivating fertile crops and producing sufficient food were often more important than defeating enemies and increasing territory and wealth. Early communities, populated by hunter-gatherers, had a very specific goal, which was to produce enough food. Each community had their own territorial boundaries and within these boundaries there were different areas: inhabited space, cultivated space for crops and/or animals, and the outside. The inhabited and cultivated areas were familiar and both safe and protected. Beyond the known space, the land was believed to be dangerous, inhabited by a variety of spiritual and corporeal dangers, including demons and ghosts, which had to be pacified.

The life cycle – both personal and agricultural – was dominated by rituals, which marked out seasons and/or events. Ploughing, sowing and harvesting all had protective, and hopefully propitious, rites. Other sorts of agricultural or food production, such as fishing and dairy work, had similar observances. Calendar customs would mark the yearly cycle; some of which were religious, such as saints' days and Easter, but others, such as Samhain and Beltane, were older. Since the weather was important to all agricultural societies, many of the rituals were associated with attempting to predict or control the weather.

The personal household or family unit was just as important as the wider community. Thus the family dwelling space was also blessed and protected by rituals and practices: most importantly the maintenance of the hearth and fire to provide warmth and the means to cook food. Human life cycle events or rites of passage were marked by special routines: marriage, fertility and conception, birth, puberty and death all had significance to the survival of the family unit. Marriage, fertility and birth were also all important for the survival of the community. Death was fundamentally important as it marked the passage from this world to the next. It was thought that the soul could linger for a time after death before moving on, and care had to be taken with the body of the departed. If a person was not buried in the correct manner or place then the soul or spirit might return as a ghost or spectre.

On a more day-to-day basis, illness and injury were also important and both their causes and cures could be attributed to magic. Although medicine and surgery from fully trained physicians and surgeons was available, it was costly and relatively rare. A more reasonable and accessible system of healing was to make a pilgrimage to shrines and other powerful sites, or to consult a local healer or charmer. These healers had special skills and knowledge that had been passed on to them either by birth or through another person: the seventh son or from mother to son and father to daughter. Some healers could only treat one specific condition, but others had a more general skill. They would use herbs, laying-on of hands, washing, blessing, and rituals using objects and words. The philosophy behind their healing was that of transference: their objective was to transfer the disease or force that caused the problem from the sufferer to another place, thing or sometimes, often accidentally, person. This, as with other elements of early-modern ritual observances, reflected the idea of limited good: that is that there was only so much good fortune to go round and that one person's good luck would result in bad luck for someone else.

The use of magic declined in Scotland for several reasons. The church played an important part in this as it sought to reduce the popularity of what it saw as a rival system of belief. Yet the early, and medieval pre-Reformation, church used the tradition of magical miracles to demonstrate its power. Holy men were seen to predict the future, control the weather, provide protection and bring help to the sick. The overlap between the two systems, therefore, could be seen as fuzzy and blurred. The Reformation, however, rejected the idea of the power of miracles and claimed that pre-Reformation church ritual was modelled on the magical form of pre-Christian tradition. Fundamental to the reformers' argument was the belief in transubstantiation. Pre-Reformation church doctrine held that the bread and wine literally turned into the body and blood of Christ. The position of the reformers was that the bread and wine was simply commemorative and symbolic rather than real. They dismissed the possibility of

5

transubstantiation as being magical and therefore impossible.

The next blow for the popularity of magic came from the intellectual changes that occurred in scientific and philosophical fields in the seventeenth and eighteenth centuries. These disciplines proposed a mechanical world-view. Descartes rejected the idea of spirits, and proposed that the body and mind were the only significant elements in our world. For a short while, magic and science had merged as a means to prove the existence of God – notably through alchemy, astrology and mathematics (it was believed that numbers had magical power). The new mechanical sciences, however, were predicated on the understanding that in order for something to be true it had to be demonstrated and tested. Nevertheless, rational science did not dominate the world-view immediately. There were still aspects of life that society could not control, such as famine, disease and weather, but as the illusion of control increased, during the eighteenth century and later, the need for magic declined.

Of course an alternative position would be to argue that it was the decline in the interest in magic that permitted the growth of rational science, rather than the other way round. To some extent neither argument is absolutely correct; just as neither religion nor science replaced magic on their own. Indeed for those who used magic as part of their daily lives, the distinction between magic, science and religion was to a large extent irrelevant. Magic had, and continued to have, a significant place in individual's lives. It offered practical procedures but at the same time provided a symbolic function. People, however, did not necessarily have to understand what they were doing. It is argued that, because of this incomplete understanding, magic was used out of ignorance. It is also claimed that there is now no place for magic in the present rational world, because modern people are no longer ignorant. Yet in the twenty-first century how many people really understand how science, electricity or the Internet works? How many accept medical advice without knowing a lot about what is happening? This is not to suggest that computers, electricity and medicine are the new magic, but rather to show that past societies were not foolish, naïve or ignorant in their acceptance of magic. Indeed, given the popularity of books like J. R. R. Tolkien's *Lord of the Rings*, J. K. Rowling's *Harry Potter* and Philip Pullman's *Dark Materials* trilogy, as well as television programmes like *Buffy the Vampire Slayer* and *Charmed* it would seem that there is an increased and increasing interest in magic and spiritual power at the moment. Scientists claim to have completed the Human Genome Project to identify every single human chromosome in order to advance genetic manipulation. This is a level of science well beyond the understanding of the majority of the population. Some could argue, indeed, this is reminiscent of the early alchemists whose quest was to find the essence of life. Most of the public, however, neither care enough to complain, nor to participate, at this level.

At different times, both churchmen and scientists have been afraid of magic. Churchmen claimed that any rival religious doctrine or belief system was based on heresy, blasphemy and ignorance – or diabolic magic. Scientists then claimed to have developed a more rational and better system than either magic or religion. Yet it is scientists who are responsible for nuclear weapons and for growing a human ear on the back of a mouse. Witches or magicians, or indeed men of God, never claimed to have 'achieved' either of these feats. Perhaps now is the time for magic to reclaim its place in the world-view, as it seems that science is becoming increasingly incomprehensible and therefore frightening and beyond the control of ordinary people.

The book has three sections: magic, witchcraft, and places of interest. In the first section general theories and principles about magic will be outlined, as will its use by early-modern society in Scotland, both as communal and private activities. The importance of different festivals and the use of rituals will be covered. The visiting of shrines and wells, and the use of amulets and talismans, will also be examined; as will the significance and power of stones. Since most of these magical customs and beliefs related to healing and good luck it is these aspects that will be explored in this part rather than harmful or adverse outcomes. The significance of healers, those individuals who practised specialised magical healing, will also be considered.

The second part of the book examines witchcraft or demonic magic. In this section, the general principles of demonic witchcraft will be outlined, explaining the difference between beneficial magic and witchcraft. This will cover harmful outcomes and bad luck that were regarded as the result of witchcraft or demonic magic. Fundamental to this was, of course, the Devil; and the significance of Satan in witchcraft belief will be examined. The Devil was not such a clear-cut grotesque figure as theologians and other writers have suggested; in many cases the Devil was more mundane and inconsequential than monstrous or spine chilling. Demonic spirits also included ghosts, and elves and fairies. Rather than being the pretty, diminutive genteel figures of Victorian sentiment, fairies were far more capricious and powerful (and tall!). The power of witches will also be covered, as will how they got their power, who they were, and how they were identified. The use of rituals and curses to invoke harmful powers and outcomes will be covered and, finally, witch hunting and trials, which were carried out in the sixteenth and seventeenth centuries, will be discussed.

The third part of the book contains information about places of interest that are associated with the different aspects of magic and witchcraft. Not all the places mentioned in the text are included in the places to visit section as many of them, particularly springs, wells and stones, have disappeared or could not be located. They may have dried up or been built over or they may not be accessible in any practical way.

Magic

What is Magic?

Magic was fundamental to people's way of life – even more so than religion – but it had different forms. On the one hand there was popular or low magic practised on an everyday level; on the other there was intellectual or high magic practised by those such as astrologers and alchemists. As mentioned above, the main types of intellectual magic were ceremonial, natural, sorcery or artificial, and demonic. Ceremonial magic involved rituals that were intended to raise the spiritual understanding of the individual. Natural magic manipulated the naturally occurring occult forces of nature to create effects and was seen as a form of science. Artificial magic or sorcery used props and conjuring to effect outcomes. Demonic magic involved the invocation of demonic or evil spirits to produce the desired outcome and was regarded as a perversion of religion.

There were private and personal, as well as public and communal, acts of magic. Individuals could perform some healing or good luck ritual in private but communities also performed seasonal ceremonies together, which were believed to provide mutual protection or benefit. The question is, of course, were these really acts of magic or did they overlap with religion? In order to address, or avoid, this perennial debate perhaps it is easier to regard all systems of belief and practice as part of a spectrum that accommodates not only magic and religion but also science, although not at the expense of any one over the other two.

One of the key differences between these three belief systems was that, although there were magical specialists who understood many secret formulae or rituals and were consulted for advice, there were also forms of magic that were practised by non-specialists. Not all magic relied on the intervention of, for want of a better word, magicians, unlike religion or science, which need the intermediary figures of priests or scientists to explain and control knowledge and, in many cases, understanding. Today, although some religions are very much based on acquiring an understanding of scriptural texts and personal enlightenment through contemplation, prayer or meditation, others rely on dogmatic rules and regulations and actively discourage understanding. Understanding might, if taken far enough, evolve into questioning. For some branches of religion this is regarded as unacceptable or even heretical, perhaps because it threatens their power and throws what might come to be regarded as dogma into doubt.

Equally mysterious is science. How many people understand more than the simplest of scientific laws and principles? Fossil fuels, nuclear fission, hydroelectric and even wind are all used to produce electricity, which 'comes out' of the sockets in most people's homes, enabling the use of computers, the Internet and email. To use these does not require understanding of the creation, conversion and storage of energy, just learning and obeying some basic rules. Perhaps many of today's citizens should try to understand more about science and scientific research, if only so that they can start to question the morality of that research. But that is another debate altogether.

Much of what was interpreted, or carried out, as magic can seem quite strange and alien to a modern audience. In order to 'explain' belief in, and practise of, magic some modern theorists have used psychological or sociological models. Both types of theories about magic were based largely on guesswork: imagining how another society thought and behaved. Belief in magic, therefore, is usually dismissed as having been primitive or irrational. That perspective is, however, unsatisfactory, since a corollary would be that magic and religion could both be seen as primitive systems of belief and thought, which would then leave science as the preferred modern system. Such a bleak option has been dismissed by sociologists such as Max Weber, who proposed that, far from being mutually exclusive, magic, religion and science are complimentary; they are different but all are equally necessary to society. All societies and cultures need the rationality and practicality of science and the here and now, and the passion of magic, religion or spirituality.

In classical writings, the word magic was applied to the practices of the magi, who were Zoroastrian priests of Persia. The Greeks knew of the existence of the magi by the fifth century BC, but neither the Greeks nor the Romans were entirely clear what they did. It was recorded that they practised astrology, healed the sick using complicated ceremonies, and generally seemed to have been interested in pursuing occult knowledge. The art of the magi, also called magical arts or magic, in reality had an imprecise meaning, but because the magi and their practices were foreign and exotic their customs evoked suspicion and apprehension mixed with curiosity. The whole concept of magic therefore developed dark and sinister connotations, albeit it was also seen as something exciting.

One of the most common uses of magic was for divination. Classical authors codified the different forms of divination using stars – astromancy, water – hydromancy, air – aeromancy, earth – geomancy, fire – pyromancy, and by consulting the dead – necromancy. Other means used to predict the future included examining the entrails of animals, the positions of stars, the flight of birds, and other signs from the natural world. Medieval philosophers and theologians regarded all of these applications and practices as essentially demonic. But then they also regarded the ordinary person who gathered herbs at sunrise or who walked their beasts through the embers of a fire as being in league with demons.

Gradually, around the thirteenth century, writers began to differentiate between what was regarded as demonic and that which could be categorised as a more acceptable form of 'natural' magic. Natural magic used the occult powers of nature, which originated from the inherent energy associated with the physical structure of, for example, stones, herbs and trees. This might come from the physical properties of an object, which could be, for example, dry, moist, hot or cold. On the other hand it could be more symbolic and relate to the shape or colour of a plant, which might indicate the condition or organ that it could cure. It was also believed that objects had animistic properties or that they had individual spirits or personalities. This is demonstrated by the beliefs associated with the mandrake plant. It was thought that mandrake had very powerful magical and curative properties as the root of the mandrake plant can sometimes resemble an upside-down human body. When the root was pulled out the ground it was believed that it would resist and cry out, and take revenge on whatever or whoever had pulled it up. To avoid any potential harm to humans, dogs would be used to pull the roots out and suffer any consequences. The mandrake root could then be used in the manufacture of medicines, often in some form of sleeping draught, although it was also believed to aid fertility and to provide protection against demonic possession. It is a strong emetic and purgative in larger quantities.

This form of magic – natural magic – was more acceptable to intellectual scholars and, for some, it was transformed into a more acceptable speciality: science. Nevertheless, many people, particularly theologians, continued to regard all forms of magic as being demonic. Even those who called themselves scientists had to be careful to avoid the criticism of the church.

Modern interpretation of magic owes much to the work of nineteenth- and twentieth-century anthropologists, in particular James G. Frazer, who developed the main principles underpinning the understanding of magical ritual and belief. Frazer's magnum opus *The Golden Bough*, was published between 1890 and 1922, and an abridged one-volume version appeared in 1922. Although Frazer has been out of fashion among anthropologists since the 1950s, some of his theories about the principles of magic are still applicable. He proposed that the theory of 'sympathetic' magic had laws of similarity and contiguity. The first principle proposed that 'like produces like' or the effect resembles the cause; the second that once something has been in contact with another object they continued to act on each other even though physical contact might have been broken. A later anthropologist, Marcel Mauss, developed another theory, that of 'antipathy', which stated that opposites work on each other.

Although the theories of sympathy and antipathy were important to the power of magic, the actions involved in the rituals on their own were equally significant. According to the work of the anthropologist Émile Durkheim, rites or rituals were of primary importance; they often came before belief and demonstrated the dominance of the community or society over the individual. Ceremonies reflected a group's need for survival, and gave people an opportunity to do something in order to control their lives. Rituals may only have offered an illusion of control; nevertheless they could provide comfort and security. It was necessary to perform the rituals in the correct order and manner, so that they would be effective. If the performance was incomplete, botched or spoiled in some way, it was believed that the ritual would be powerless, although it was not always explained what had worked and what had not. Since magic could not always explain why something did or did not work, opponents argued it did not have any solid rationale or theory. Even if magic did not appear to have rigid terms and theories, it was neither chaotic nor whimsical. It was firmly based in the social and cultural environment of the time and place; and, despite attacks by the church and later scientists, it was central to daily life.

Most of the magical rituals that were practised by ordinary communities and individuals were apotropaic: that is they were intended to prevent or repel evil. Many were rites of purification, sacrifice, and blessing. Despite criticisms by churchmen and others, most magic was not used to cause deliberate harm. Magic was essentially neutral and the effect, whether good or bad, was usually the result of the particular intentions of the user. Undoubtedly magic was used to elicit deliberate harm – there are cases where magic was used as means of attempted murder – but, due to the principles of transference and limited good, harm was more often caused by one person's good luck accidentally resulting in another person's misfortune. Of course, in order to counteract perceived misfortune, or to prevent it occurring, communal acts of apotropaic magic, especially calendar customs and rites of passage, were carried out to maintain a sense of community and participation. There was therefore a cycle of magic.

USES OF MAGIC

Intentional harm, or maleficium, through the use of witchcraft will be discussed later. This section will consider non-harmful, or even beneficial, uses of magic rather than the malefice associated with demonic magic or witchcraft. The commonest beneficial uses of magic include healing, good luck, divination, finding lost goods, and love magic. In England and elsewhere in Europe, the term cunning-folk, or wise-men or wise-women, was used to describe those whose magical practice included divination, locating stolen or lost items and love magic. Charmers were those who offered advice and help about particular ailments or conditions; they used healing magic. These charmers had limited healing powers, which were conferred on them by circumstances of birth, the acquisition of healing objects, or the knowledge of healing rituals for specific conditions. In England there was a two-fold division between those who practised healing (charmers) and the other applications (cunning or wise-folk). In Scotland the divisions were more ambiguous and the terms charming and charmers was often used to accommodate both.

Illness was an everyday occurrence and there were various theories about causes and cures – some of them held by elite physicians and surgeons, others held at a more personal or popular level. Explanations could be based on natural, supernatural, religious, magical and even social causes. One elite natural explanation was that contagion could cause illness. It was understood that exposure to certain diseases, such as leprosy and plague, could result in more infection. Town councils and university-trained physicians developed policies of isolation to help reduce the spread. This was not, however, the only possible explanation for the causes of these diseases. A religious interpretation was that illness could have been sent as a form of punishment for sin or unacceptable behaviour: epidemics of plague and leprosy were often described as

16

punishment from God. In order to prevent or limit the spread of these kinds of disease, populations were encouraged to pray and ask divine forgiveness. Another explanation was based on the idea that an illness was transferred – not only through direct exposure, but also by the movement of the disease entity from one being to another. This meant that illnesses could be transferred deliberately or accidentally – and without any direct contact.

The explanations of contagion and transference can both be seen as attempts to describe infection by microorganisms – the latter being something that is understood by twenty-first century society. According to elite medical opinion, other factors also affected health, some of which might be less well understood today. The climate or environment, the lunar, astral and planetary alignments, and humoral imbalance were all very important, both in causing and in the treatment of disease. The medicines offered by physicians in the sixteenth and seventeenth centuries was based on classical medical texts, such as those of Hippocrates and Galen, the fathers of ancient medicine. Some of the treatments recommended were unpleasant, and would be unacceptably painful to a modern-day patient. The basic principle that informed all procedures was the restoration of humoral balance by first purging the patient using expectorants, enemas, emetics and bleeding, followed by restoration with tonics. The four humours were blood, yellow bile, black bile, and phlegm; and they were regarded as fundamental to the working of the body. It was believed that any disorder in their balance would result in illness, and treatments were designed to restore harmony. The purging and bleeding that was recommended was often distressing and debilitating, and required the administration of tonics and other supplements to restore strength.

Although the popular explanation of transference was associated with ideas about movement from one body to another, it was also related to being bewitched. As has already been mentioned, illness could be transferred accidentally during the removal of bewitchment from an affected individual. Deliberate witchcraft and revenge could, however, also cause illness – perhaps through the use of the evil eye or droch shuil – or the breaking of some taboo. It was also believed that spirits and elves or fairies could cause illnesses, either at their own volition or at the request of another person.

With all these various explanations of cause and effect, different communities treated different kinds of diseases in different ways. Thus most communities had levels of disease: those they could treat at home by themselves, and those for which they would seek outside help, either through religious means or from some local or well-known folk healer. For those who had a certain amount of wealth and status, there was another option, which may have replaced the others: the services of trained physicians or surgeons. The majority of the population, however, could not afford to seek this 'professional' help. Even those who could use the services of a physician or surgeon often also sought the advice of local folk healers. People were just as likely to use a combination of treatments and recommendations in the past as they do now – or at least hedge their bets. Today people will often minister to themselves using information from family and friends, self-help pages, books, television shows or internet sites, and advice from pharmacists – as well as general medical practitioners. There is of course also a wide range of complimentary medical services that are now available: homeopathy, herbalism, chiropractic and Chinese medicine, although the latter is in fact as old as Hippocratic and Galenic medicine. Due to the ever-changing quality of medical services that are currently being offered in Britain, general practitioners are now often one of the last options to be consulted rather than the first. Rather than being original and alternative, perhaps people are simply repeating behaviour more reminiscent of past centuries.

Since folk healers were so prevalent, who were they and what did they do? Folk healers had a gift for healing that they could acquire in various ways. Some of them were born with it, or acquired it due to the circumstances of their birth. This included those who were deaf and dumb, seventh sons and daughters, people with red hair, trained gardeners or blacksmiths, individuals who were born with a caul, had a breech birth, and even the survivor of a set of twins. Others acquired it through an older person, often passed contrasexually from female to male and vice versa, perhaps through a whispered secret charm or the ownership of a special item.

MAGICAL SPIRITS

E xplanations for healing knowledge and skill varied. A feature of some European societies was to have the 'gift' bestowed by some supernatural power. For some, the supernatural power took the form of saints or angels, but in Scotland there were several cases of folk healers who claimed that the fairies had given them their healing powers. In 1597, Andrew Man, from Aberdeen, said the Queen of Elves gave him his skill of healing after he had helped deliver her child. Alison Pearson, from Fife, said her 'uncle', whom she claimed had travelled in the East and learnt the black arts, took her to fairy meetings. The fairies gave her the power to heal but also punished her physically – she lost the power of one side of her body – when she tried to resist them or tell other people about her experiences. Bessie Dunlop, from Ayrshire, had a similar relationship with the fairies as Andrew Man. She had given the Queen of Elves a drink and in return the fairy sent Bessie a fairy helper – called Thomas Reid – who helped and advised her. Bessie then developed a reputation as a healer and was consulted by many people for help.

Healing knowledge was not the only power that could be passed on by fairies; other skills were often said to have been gifted, although sometimes at a price. There is a hill known as Cnoc na Piobaireachd or knoll of the piping, on Eigg. Local tradition claimed that young men gathered there to practise and learn new tunes, which they could hear being played through the ground. The MacCrimmons, who were the hereditary pipers to the MacLeods of Dunvegan, had a silver chanter that they said had been given to them by a fairy lover. Another chanter – this time black – belonged to the Chattans. It was said to have been given to a MacPherson, pipers to the Chattans, by his fairy lover.

Another skill that fairies could transmit was prophecy. Thomas the Rhymer or True Thomas – whose real name was

Thomas of Ercildoune – was a thirteenth-century poet and seer. It was said that Thomas met the Queen of Fairies on the Eildon Hills near Melrose. Thomas followed the queen after kissing her on the lips, and he had to serve her for seven years. While in the fairy realm, the queen gave Thomas a magical apple, which was the source of his ability to predict the future honestly – hence his second epithet, True Thomas. Although Thomas of Ercildoune is credited with writing *The Romance of Sir Tristam*, he was better known for his prophecies. It is said that Thomas predicted the crowning of Robert the Bruce in 1306 and the defeat at Flodden in 1513. Since many of the prophecies did not appear in print until the fifteenth century, it is, therefore, very difficult to prove their authenticity. It is interesting to note that Andrew Man, in his confessions about his association with the fairies, described meeting both Thomas the Rhymer and James IV, who was killed at Flodden, as ghosts at a fairy meeting. Although he did not say when this meeting occurred, it was presumably in the mid- to late-sixteenth century.

Not all visitors to the realm of the fairies were able to return so freely. The ballad of *Tam Lin* is allegedly about the son of Thomas Randolph, the Earl of Moray, who was a companion of Robert the Bruce. The ballad suggests that Tam Lin was a changeling who had been stolen by the fairies as a child. Later he meets a human girl, Janet, at Carterhaugh, and they conceive a child. In order to bring Tam back from the fairies Janet has to defeat the fairy queen by holding on to Tam during a number of increasingly ferocious dangers. A well near Carterhaugh, known as Tamlane's Well and where one of the incidents in the ballad is thought to take place, can be visited, although it has been filled in.

Not all traditions associated with fairy lore were so hazardous. The MacLeods of Dunvegan have in their possession the Fairy Flag or Am Bratach Sith – said to have belonged to the fairy wife of one of the clan chiefs who remained in the mortal realm for twenty years before returning to her own world. Another version, however, claims that the wife of the chief interrupted a fairy singing a lullaby to the chief's son. The fairy woman, who was wearing green, had wrapped the child in a cloth – possibly she was about to steal the child – fled when the chief's wife cried out, but left the cloth behind. Yet another version has it that the fabric was given to a MacLeod who destroyed an evil spirit when he was on crusade. The fabric is Middle Eastern silk but is dated from between the fourth and seventh centuries, well before the crusades. Whichever version is true, and it may be none of these, for generations it has been claimed that the flag has special powers to protect the MacLeod clan. It was said that the flag was draped over the wedding bed of the chief to ensure a fertile marriage. According to legend it was unfurled at the battles of Glendale in 1490 and Trumpan in 1580. It has not been used in such a manner since then, as it was only to be used this way three times. Pictures of the flag were, however, carried during the Second World War by airmen who were members of the MacLeod clan.

There are a number of Scottish place names that make reference to fairies. Sometimes these may have actually have been prehistoric chambered cairns or later iron-age souterrains. Although descriptions of fairies often make no mention of their size, and those that do infer that they are the same size as humans, there is, and was, a common misconception that fairies lived underground and were small. Later generations did not understand the purpose of these underground passageways and chambers and so gave them names such as fairy knowe or hillock; thus merging oral folk legend with the physical environment. There are many Cnoc an t-Suidhe throughout Scotland, in Skye, Perthshire, Aberdeenshire, Mull and Moray. The mountain known as Schiehallion in the Grampians translates as the fairy hill of the Grampians, and Glenshee, in Perthshire, means fairy glen. Sith is Gaelic for fairy or supernatural; and banshee means fairy woman from ban-sith.

One of the most detailed accounts of fairy lore in Scotland

was, interestingly, written by a minister. The Reverend Robert Kirk who was minister of Balquhidder from 1664 to 1685, then at Aberfoyle in Stirlingshire from 1685 until his death in 1692, published *The Secret Commonwealth of Elves, Fauns and Fairies* in 1691. In it, Kirk described fairyland, elfin society, their appearance and their powers. According to Kirk, fairies were something, and somewhere, between man and angel. Their bodies were light and ephemeral, like condensed cloud. They were agile and swift, and could appear and disappear at will. Other features, such as green clothing, blonde or golden hair, and silver bells, reflected ideas about fairies that were part of the culture of the time. These ideas have been transmitted down through generations and have become fixed in folk memory, such as their ability to convert ordinary water into fine wine, hard bread into lightest cake, rough thread into softest cloth, and beautiful music from discordant notes. Kirk died on the Doon Hill, and was buried in the cemetery at Kirkton of Aberfoyle. Some say that his mortal body was seized by the fairies, and is imprisoned at in an old Scots pine tree which grows in a clearing on the hill.

There were also other spiritual beings mentioned in Scottish folk legend. These included brownies and gruagach. Brownies, which also feature in other European cultures, were domestic spirits who were human sized, often wild and shaggy, and derive their lowland name from their dark complexion. Brownies also seem to have been mostly male. James VI described brownies in his book *Daemonologie* which he wrote at the end of the sixteenth century. He described a kind of spirit that did not do evil, but did necessary turns in the house. He wrote: 'this spirit they call brownie in our language, who appeared like a rough man. Yea some were so blinded as to believe that their house was all the sonsier [luckier] that such spirits resorted there'.

Brownies were associated with families and households, usually of some wealth, and would appear at night to undertake or complete any unfinished domestic tasks. They do not appear to have worked for food or other rewards, and could be easily offended. Brownies were also known as Whippitie Stourie, and were often associated with spinning and weaving, although, like Rumpelstiltskin in the fairy tale, they could be deceitful.

A number of castles, houses and even farms were said to have had a resident brownie, including Ardincaple, near Helensburgh, Claypotts Castle near Dundee, Dunskey Castle near Portpatrick in Galloway, Invergarry Castle in the Great Glen, Lochnell House, near Oban, Castle Lachlan near Strachur, Dolphinston Tower near Jedburgh, Cranshaws Tower near Duns in the Borders, and Noltland Castle on Westray in Orkney. The Balfour family built Noltland and it was said a brownie, the spirit of an old man, assisted the household by clearing roads, helping with boats and other general tasks. The brownie left the family when they abandoned the castle in the eighteenth century. The brownie of Claypotts left the family when a servant refused to let it help. At Dolphinston the brownie left because it was given an unsuitable present, and at Cranshaws because an ungrateful servant had criticised its work.

Although most brownies were described as male and were rather ragged in appearance, a few were female. The brownie who helped at Skipness near Tarbert in Argyll was said to have had golden hair and wore a green dress. Her appearance bears some resemblance to that of a gruagach. Gruagach were said to be the spirits of women who had died in childbirth or who had been enchanted in some other way – perhaps they were human women who had been stolen by the fairies but, unlike Tam Lin or Thomas the Rhymer, had not managed to escape. Unlike brownies who were often linked to a family and would sometimes follow them if they moved, gruagach were tied to a specific place. They were known for the help around the household and in particular help in the dairy. Gruagach were sometimes given offerings, usually of milk, in return for their help. Again, like the brownie, gruagach could be easily offended and if the reward was not left they could seek revenge by causing chaos: the cows could be untied, the milk spilt or spoiled, the corn broken before it was ground. An offering of milk left for the gruagach would often be left at a special place – sometimes a stone or Clach na Gruagach (stone of the gruagach). They were relatively common on Skye and Tiree. Caisteal Camus on Skye was said to have had a gruagach, as did Castle Loch Heylipol on Tiree and Dunstaffnage near Oban.

Gruagach were also associated with predicting the fortunes of a family or its members: if a family was due good news then the gruagach would appear happy, but if it was bad news then she would appear sad and weeping.

MAGICAL HEALERS

Although fairies were said to be able to pass on healing skills, a more frequent explanation given by healers was that their mother, grandmother, father, a person who was known to them in some other way, or even a priest had given them their knowledge. A common feature of these explanations was that the person who had passed on the secret was dead. This method of transmission was not uncommon, and perpetuated the idea that this was a special gift, known only to a few, and which was to be given respect.

Some healers could only treat specific conditions. A well-known example is that of seventh sons who were believed to be able to cure scrofula (lymphatic tuberculosis). Interestingly, another kind of person who was believed to have the power to treat scrofula was the monarch. Being touched by kings and queens was believed to have curative powers, and it was recorded that people would make a form of pilgrimage in order to be touched by the royal hand. Some monarchs may, however, have been less than thrilled at the prospect of touching hundreds of their subjects, and offered royal coins or tokens instead.

Other specific healing skills included those who had been born breech or those who were deaf and/or unable to speak. People who were born breech could treat sufferers from bad backs, and those who were 'deaf and dumb' were consulted in order to identify the location of lost or stolen goods.

The kind of advice that folk healers offered included the use of physical objects, actions and/or words. The objects that were mentioned included clothing, metal, herbs, salt, eggs, wood, water, thread or twine, and even animals. People tied toads round the necks of their sheep because they thought it would cure them of braxy or breakshaw, an intestinal disease that affected sheep, which was usually fatal. Live toads were also buried at the threshold of an afflicted person's house in the belief that the disease entity would be transferred to the object. A similar belief informed the ritual of burying a live cockerel, particularly a black one, at the site where an epileptic took their first fit. It was thought that the demon that caused the epilepsy would be transferred to the bird and the human would be cured.

Sometimes the rituals that were to be carried could be quite complicated. Margery Kerr was told to get a cat from her neighbour's house, although she was not to ask for it. She was then to pass it three times around and under her cow and, after the third time, she was to throw it out the door. Then she was to take her left shoe and pass it round the cow three times the same way and to slap the cow each time. Next she was to take some of the cow's milk and throw it out of the house through a hole where no light could come in. Then more of the milk was to be taken to a march, or boundary, burn, where she was to mix it with some water and bring it home and put it in the cow's ear three times. This was all done in order to cure the cow and, according to Margery, it worked, although she also claimed that the unnamed condition was transferred to another of her animals as a result of the ritual.

It was not only whole animals that were used in healing rituals. Bits of animal could also be used. In the Western Islands in the seventeenth century, locals used girdles made of sealskin to help their sciatica or back pain. It was not only magical medicine or folk remedies that used animals or animal products in their treatments. Some medicinal recipes prescribed by physicians of the time, included ingredients such as peacock droppings, horse dung, and even whole mice, which were usually made more palatable by the addition of sugar and wine. On the whole, magic treatments were seemingly no more disgusting or disagreeable than those offered by orthodox medical practitioners.

Fairies or elves may have been credited with passing on

healing knowledge to some individuals, but they were more generally regarded with suspicion and not a little fear. Fairies were capricious beings and, although Scottish folklore has many tales of individuals benefiting from their encounters with fairies (such as acquiring the ability to play the pipes or fiddle extremely well), the stories are also careful to stress the dangers associated with them. Fairies could bestow magical powers, but they could also punish if they were offended.

In particular, fairies could steal newly-born babies and substitute one of their own offspring to be nursed by a human mother, or they could take a nursing mother with them to their own realm and hold her captive in order to feed their own children. If a baby changed its behaviour, particularly if it stopped thriving or growing, it was thought to have been replaced by a changeling – it was claimed Tam Lin had been taken and replaced by a changeling. If it was suspected that the human baby had been stolen then 'exorcising' the fairy – or scaring it away using fire – was a common procedure. It was believed that the fairy changeling would be so frightened by the fire that it would flee and the human baby returned to its family. In one case, Margaret Dickson told one of her neighbours to bake some meal into a bread or biscuit. He was then to take empty eggshells and put the bread and eggshells in front of the fire. At midnight he was to go nine times round his house then come inside and say 'Rise up also and go, in the Devil's name, and give me my daughter again'. She said that if the child was going to return then the eggshells and bread would be gone, but if not, then they would remain.

A less complicated changeling ritual involved putting a cradle containing a sick child on the hearth after first taking the fire out. Another version of this, albeit one that was more dangerous, involved putting the baby in the fire, although how often this was done is unclear.

Changeling belief continued after the Reformation and into the seventeenth century, but gradually the concept disappeared, although the sentiment behind it continued for much longer. In some cases, it would appear to have been used as a distressing excuse for abuse. In the late nineteenth century, Bridget Cleary, from Connel in Ireland, was thought to be a changeling – in this case it would appear to have been an adult one rather than a newborn baby. Bridget was held over a fire by her husband, and other relatives, and tragically died of her injuries. Those involved were accused of murder.

One theory about the phenomenon of changeling-babies, which fits a modern-day medical model, is that of failure to thrive. Small, underweight babies who are often restless, who feed poorly and often have absorption difficulties, appear to resemble the descriptions of changelings found in older testimonies. Of course, it is impossible to identify accurately whether this is true or not. Even today the belief has not entirely disappeared: newborn babies are often slipped a small silver coin or were even given a silver brooch because silver would protect them from the fairies. Although the reason for doing something may be forgotten, the practice itself often continues.

Herbs or plants were sometimes mentioned as part of healing – although perhaps not as often as we might imagine. It may have been that other – more symbolic or magical – ingredients seem to have been more significant to the idea of witchcraft belief and practice, whereas knowledge of herbs was less threatening and more acceptable. That does not mean that herbs were never used as part of magic. Those that were used seem to have been quite typical of herbal medicine in general. Marion Sprott advised John Murray to eat aniseed and his health improved as a result. Aniseed has a general calming effect, particularly on the digestive system. Other herbs that were recommended included the usual foxglove, plantain, St John's wort, groundsel, ragwort and so forth.

Some form of action or ritual seems to have been important to magical healing practices. The sort of actions that were recommended for healing included going to a well or river, going round a tree or a house a specific number of times, or passing through a piece of yarn. Turning or passing over something has already been mentioned for treating a cow, but a similar action was used to treat mawturning, or nausea, in children. Mothers were told to turn their children three times head over heels between barn doors or round an oak tree. This may have been to make the child vomit, which ultimately might have made them feel better, although this was not explicitly stated. The significant markers in this procedure are the number three, the turning, and the oak. Although oak, as a plant (leaves or bark), was used to treat conditions such as diarrhoea, haemorrhage, dysentery, sore throat and bleeding gums and piles, its significance was also symbolic and related to the power of its size and strength. Although hazel and rowan trees were generally more important, fires of oak wood were burnt at festival times and oak copses were believed to have been used as places of worship. Groves of oak trees were revered by the Druids.

Sometimes words were used as part of a healing ritual, and this often meant spoken verses that resembled prayers. For example, 'God teach me to pray to put this ill away, out of the flesh, blood and bane, into the earth and cold stane, and nevir to come again, in God's name'. Or 'The closing which St Comrie gave ye, cattle which St Patrick left in the field, noe thief shall touch them in the fields, they shall not be lost in the waters or drowned in the seas. From rocks and weather the barefooted swift thieves they shall be down, in the Cross of Earnan and rise in the Cross of Christ till they come again in peace'. This latter verse was reported to have been used by Anne Buy from Killearnan parish in 1732 to prevent cattle from straying or getting stolen; Earnan was a local saint.

The use of verses such as these was sometimes troublesome, both for the users themselves and the church authorities. After 1560, the official church in Scotland was Protestant, rather than Catholic. The reformed church was disturbed by the use of ritual, which it regarded as being superstitious and ignorant. Although the reformed church permitted prayer, when it was associated with a ritual it was too reminiscent of pre-Reformation, or Catholic, worship. Throughout the seventeenth century, the church in Scotland attempted to outlaw these practices and investigated their continued use by members of the congregation. On occasion, individuals would be called before a kirk session to account for their actions and the intention behind them. There was a fine line between carrying out healing rituals – sometimes called charming – and witchcraft, the consequences of which could be very serious.

Practices such as divination, finding lost goods, and love magic were also awkward for the church. There was, however, still a need for them and so their use continued, despite the threat of censure. As late as 1697 the Dumfries presbytery was consulted for advice about a case of charming from Caerlaverock, which was referred to as the 'turning of the key'. This incident involved the use of the Bible and a key. Ownership of a Bible – the written version of God's word – was more common by the end of the seventeenth century than in previous centuries, but it was still relatively rare. Indeed, although literacy was quite good in some parts of Scotland, it was by no means universal This meant that the Bible had a great deal of symbolic power, due both to its content and also its physical presence. A group of three men had gone for a drink to William Irons' house. While they were drinking, one of them, William Richardson, had his sack stolen, which had contained some cheese and herring. The third man, John Ferguson, then claimed that he would be able to identify the thief and asked Irons to bring him two Bibles. Initially Irons said he did not have one but, after Ferguson threatened him with 'bloodie work', managed to find the required number. Then, placing a key between pages of the Bible, Ferguson read three verses from Psalm 50, verse 18-20. 'When thou sawest a thief, then thou consentedst with him and hast been partaker with adulterers. Thou givest thy mouth to evil, and thy tongue frameth deceit. Thou sittest and speakest against thy brother, thou slanderest thine own mother's son'. It was claimed that he named all the locals individually before he read the extract from the Bible and when he came to the name of one local man – William McKinnell – the key and the Bible turned over and fell off the table. They carried this out three times in order to confirm their suspicions. Ferguson confessed to the presbytery that he had carried out the ritual and that he had some knowledge of charming, but claimed he did not know there was anything evil in what he had done. Although the church authorities were concerned about what had been done, they did not categorise these actions as witchcraft. Ferguson was ordered to stand at the pillar in his church at Caerlaverock and be sharply rebuked – a much more preferable option to capital punishment.

The identification of stolen or lost goods was also often associated with people who were deaf or who were 'deaf and dumb'. These individuals would be consulted for information about the thief or how to retrieve their property, but unfortunately the records do not always indicate how the information was communicated. Presumably some form of sign language was used, or possibly the individual could write even if they could not speak. It is unlikely that these people made a good living – in other words getting paid money – from their 'skill' but they may have supplemented their income. It would also seem that their reputation could be quite widespread. During the seventeenth century, people would travel from other parts of East Lothian to Ormiston to consult a 'dumb boy', and to Pencaitland to see the 'dumb woman', about finding their lost property. Reputations often spread beyond just local areas; it was noted that people from Yester in East Lothian travelled to the Canongate near Edinburgh to seek the advice of a man there. Like many aspects of magical belief, the practice did not disappear completely: in the nineteenth century it was reported that a deaf and dumb fortune-teller travelled around the west of Scotland using a slate and chalk to communicate with his clients.

Another method of prognostication, used to identify

suspects, was the use of the sieve (or riddle) and shears. This was often known as 'turning the riddle'. The shears were thrust through the riddle and held aloft, then the names of suspects would be recited and if the riddle turned or fell off the shears then the guilty party would be identified. Again, throughout the seventeenth and eighteenth centuries, the church investigated its use and often reprimanded all of those involved. This ritual was not unique to Scotland as its use was recorded throughout Europe.

Divination could also be used in relation to healing; not so much as a means to heal but a method of identifying the trouble or predicting the outcome of an illness. Molten lead was held over the sick person then dropped in water. If the lead congealed into the identifiable shape of an organ or part of the body then it was believed that that was the part that was affected. Another method of predicting the outcome, particularly in the case of sick children, was measuring or 'metting' as it was described. Healers recorded that they were asked to mett a child in order to detect if it would recover or not. In some parts of Europe and the USA, routine measuring of a child was thought to stunt its growth. This may have been because measuring was something that was done to a sick child, and if a healthy child was measured then it would bring bad luck.

In Scotland, a belt, or some form of yarn, was stretched from the head to the feet, around the waist, or around the affected part. Bessie Graham used this operation a number of times. She was requested to 'met the belt' for several children in order to predict whether they would recover or not – and in most cases she seemed to have predicted a rather negative prognosis. She told Andrew Arolls that there was no remedy for his child. Agnes Johnston described how she took her sick child to Bessie for some help and advice. She said that Bessie 'tuik the belt and mettit it, muttering some speiches, with greit ganting, eftir which she [Bessie] told the said Agnes that the child was seik and wald not leive [live]'. Her prediction proved correct. Janet Cunningham's child, however, improved after Bessie had metted the belt. Cunningham was also advised by Bessie to pray for her child, which she did and, in this case, the child recovered.

Bessie Stevenson from Stirling, who was tried for witchcraft in 1659, described how she would identify, and predict, the outcome, for the 'heart fevers' using a similar method. She would wrap a belt and two threads around the sick person's chest. One thread was on the outside of the belt, the other on the inside and if the person had the fever then both threads would end up on the same side.

Another form of magic that was used was love magic; often it was really just another type of divination used to identify potential future lovers or partners, rather than a means to procure the affections of the object of desire. This form of divination was sometimes carried out at a special time of the year, particularly Hallowe'en. The peel of an apple would be thrown over the shoulder in the hope that it would assume the shape of the initial letter in a future partner's name; this is still done today. Sleeping with flowers or a mirror underneath a pillow was believed to mean that the loved one would appear in a person's dreams.

One method that was employed to secure someone's affection, rather than simply dream about them, was to steal a love token to use as part of a sympathetic magical ritual. Often this was a pubic hair. John Fian, one of those accused during the North Berwick witch trials of 1590, tried to persuade one of his pupils to bring him a pubic hair from his older sister, who had attracted Fian's attention. The boy told his mother who, it was claimed, substituted his sister's hair with a hair from the tail of a young cow. It is said that Fian carried out his magical rituals using the hair from the cow and, as a result, ended up being pursued by a love-sick heifer rather than the girl of his dreams.

Festivals and Rituals

F estivals were very important occasions for carrying out a number of ritual observances – and not only those related to divination. The yearly seasons were very important to a mostly agricultural society like early-modern Scotland – this included fishing as well as land-based work. They affected people's lives and their work and, as one season moved into the next, there were celebrations and rituals to observe in order to ensure good luck for the following few months.

Many of the festivals shared common features, but other elements were particular to individual ceremonies. For many of them the whole of the twenty-four hour period – midnight to midnight – was important, but for others the hours before midnight were particularly meaningful. It was believed that supernatural spirits were at their most powerful at these times, and humans at their most vulnerable. Many of the community celebrations included fire rituals and some form of offering to placate the spirits. The bonfire, or need-fire, provided personal as well as communal protection and good luck. Household fires were re-kindled from the communal bonfire; embers from it were taken home as a good luck talisman. Beasts and humans were sained (purified) by being passed through – walking or jumping over – the embers or walking around the bonfire in a sunwise direction or deiseil. Fertility was another important elements of the rituals, and this was often demonstrated by offerings, often in the form of libations of milk or other drinks.

The Celtic quarter days that were celebrated in Scotland were Imbolc in February, Beltane in May, Lugnasad in August, and Samhain in November. The solstices associated with winter – Yule – and summer – Midsummer – were also important. Christianity later integrated these earlier pre-Christian festivals into the Christian calendar, and either replaced them completely or incorporated them into a, sometimes, longer

Christian festival. Thus Imbolc, the feast of the Celtic goddess of spring, became St Bride's Day; Lugnasad, the feast of Lugh, became Lammas; Samhain, the feast of the dead, became All Saint's Day (the day after Hallowe'en); Midsummer became St John's Day; and Yule became Christmas. Some of the days for the ceremonies were also changed when the calendar was altered in 1752. Eleven days were effectively lost so that the calendar would correspond to the seasons more accurately.

The Celtic year started with the festival of Beltane, 1 May, which was associated with the feast of the Celtic god Bel who was ruler of the underworld. It was the least Christianised Celtic festival, although the later Christian feast of the Invention of the Cross or Rood Day was celebrated on 3 May. Bel was associated with renewal and birth: the fertility of the land and growing of crops, as well as personal fecundity. In seventeenth-century Scotland, it was common to collect south-running water on Beltane day and sprinkle the ground with it. Animals were then taken over the water in order to protect them and ensure fertility for the next year. Washing the face (to improve looks and beauty) in dew from Holyrood Park in Edinburgh remained popular at dawn on the first of May, although this used to be done with water from St Anthony's Well.

Thomas Pennant, a writer who travelled around Scotland in the eighteenth century, recorded another protection ritual carried out at Beltane. He observed that: 'farmers carefully preserve their cattle against witchcraft by placing boughs of the mountain ash [rowan] and honeysuckle in their cows' houses on 2nd May'. Animals were also passed through hoops of rowan for the same purpose.

Rogation (a Christian ceremony to bless crops) rituals were also often performed at this time. These took the form of protective processions around community fields and boundaries, and later coalesced into Riding of the Marches or Common Riding ceremonies, which are still carried out today in some Border towns. Some of them are carried out in a traditional manner, but others have been reinvented or have adapted and introduced new features or variations.

Many of the Ridings are now held in June and each are held in a different week. The custom now is that representatives from each town attend the neighbouring ceremonies as a gesture of support and friendliness rather than one of rivalry. Callants or Callands or Standard Bearers – male riders – from Hawick, Langholm, Lauder, Peebles, Dumfries and Selkirk all participate in the others' processions. The practice extends to Lanark and even Musselburgh in East Lothian.

Midsummer, or the Eve of the feast of St John the Baptist, was also associated with fertility. Herbs associated with St John, especially St John's wort, were gathered, as they were believed to be especially effective if picked at this time. Midsummer fires were still burnt in Aberdeenshire, Moray, Perthshire, Ayrshire and the Borders in the eighteenth century, despite the criticism of the reformed church. In Orkney and Shetland the midsummer festival is known as Johnsmas, and was still being celebrated in the twentieth century. Part of the Shetland ritual was to make milkgruel – porridge made with milk instead of water – on the fire.

The month of August marked the festival of Lugnasad or Lammas and commemorated the beginning of the harvest season. Some areas still hold fairs to mark Lammas, notably Kirkwall and St Andrews. This was a vitally important time for agricultural communities; and both the start of harvest, often coinciding with midsummer, and its completion, were observed. The right kind of weather at the right time was important, and prayers would be offered and thanks given when it had been accomplished satisfactorily. In some areas, a pleuch, or plough, feast was observed to commemorate the first ploughing of the season. In many societies, the last sheaf collected was significant – the cailleach or old woman, which was the name given to the last sheaf, was regarded as a good luck charm. It could be fed to the animals, baked in special cake, or kept as an amulet to provide protection for the household over the coming year. Alternatively in some areas, particularly Barra, the first meal that was harvested was made into a bannock, as it was also believed to be propitious.

It was also regarded as a gesture of good luck to leave a part of the crop in the field as a sort of offering. This was left behind for the spirits – sometimes the fairies – or demons. In Scotland, this was sometimes referred to as the guid man or good man. Sometimes a small area of the field, left uncultivated, would be dedicated to the 'good man'. By leaving part of the field, it was hoped that this would mean that the rest of the land would prosper. It was claimed by some that the good man might have been the Devil and the piece of land was sometimes called the good man's croft or plot.

A similar belief is reflected by a practice reported in sixteenth-century Aberdeenshire: areas of land were measured (mett) and stones put at the corners. This was to ensure that animals would be protected from lungsocht (a bovine lung disease). It was said that this was done for the 'hynd knicht' who, it was claimed, was a spirit. This may have been another name for the good man or Devil.

Samhain or All Saints (1 November) and All Souls (2 November) marked the start of winter and commemorated the dead. In England the November festivity was replaced by the celebration of the discovery of the Gunpowder plot in 1603, but the activities associated with Guy Fawkes' or Bonfire Night were not new.

As households prepared for winter, the fire festival Hallowe'en was celebrated. As it marked another move from one season to another, the spirits that had helped over the past quarter had to be offered thanks. It was also associated with darkness, witches and dangerous spirits, so was a hazardous time. Special cakes or bannocks were baked, and games and rituals carried out. As discussed earlier, divination rituals were celebrated at this time, some of which involved the use of corn or eggs: egg whites were dropped into a glass of water. Other means of fortune telling involved winding a ball of yarn or the burning of nuts.

According to the traveller Martin Martin, on Lewis, near Eoropie on the north of the island, locals made sacrifices to the sea-god Shony at Hallowe'en. They would brew ale and, after sunset, would take the ale out into the sea saying, 'Shony, I give you this cup of ale, hoping that you'll be so kind as to send up plenty of sea-ware for enriching out ground for the ensuing year'. The ale was then thrown into the sea and the community would go to the church where they would observe a short period of silence. Once the candle on the altar had been extinguished they would all go to the fields and indulge in a night of singing, dancing, and revelry. It was believed that this ceremony would ensure enough seaweed to fertilise the ground so that there would be good growth of crops.

The winter solstice or Yule marked the start of a new year, particularly in the Christian calendar, and further renewal. The celebration of Yule was a longer festival and incorporated a number of activities including Christmas, Hogmanay and the New Year. Rituals were carried out to ensure fertility, and also to divine the success of the following year. Good or bad luck for the following year could be determined by the first visitor to a house on New Year's day: tall, dark, handsome and male were considered best; a short red-haired woman was unwelcome. The symbolism of the gifts that visitors carried was related to the success of the household: corn, oats, grass and water were all believed to guarantee a plentiful supply during the following year. These gifts were later replaced with coal and shortbread, but the symbolism was much the same: fuel and food for the household for the following year.

Divination rituals were also observed at Yule, including the making of Yule sowans. Sowans was a kind of porridge made from oat husks and meal, which were steeped in water for about a week. The mixture was drained and left to ferment, then boiled and eaten like porridge. At Yule, items like a ring, button and penny were stirred into the sowans before being distributed among the company. This kind of ritual is continued today by mixing lucky charms into a Christmas pudding.

Although Christmas was important from a Christian perspective, for many it was really New Year that was more important. Because of the change in calendar in the eighteenth century, some New Year festivities – notably the burning of the clavie at Burghead – now take place on 11 January rather than on 31 December. The clavie is a half tar barrel mounted on a six-foot long fisherman's pole. The fuel consists of broken cask staves and bits of tarred wood. Once the clavie is lit it is paraded through the town to the nearby hill – the Doorie – where it is incorporated into a larger bonfire. The clavie is then broken up and the embers and pieces of burnt wood are gathered as good luck charms or talismans. In Stonehaven, New Year is celebrated by the whirling of fiery balls.

Up-Helly-Aa, or Uphalieday or Uphalimes, was the festival of Epiphany or the twelfth day after Christmas. The king or queen of the Bene was the individual in who found a bean in their portion of Twelfth Night cake. The festival of Up-Helly-Aa is now more associated with the Shetland Viking fire festival celebrated in Lerwick. Shetlanders observed Twelfth Night as a general Yule-related holiday, but in the nineteenth century the inhabitants of Lerwick extended the celebrations to include the burning of tar barrels – like Burghead. By the 1870s, the local authorities felt that the festivities were getting out of hand and moved the event to the end of the month, rather than on 6 January. Guising and a torch-lit parade were also introduced. By 1877 Up-Helly-Aa, as it was now known, incorporated some more distinctly Viking-type themes as a means to assert Shetland's Norse heritage and demonstrate a separate cultural identity from mainland Scotland. In the 1880s, a replica longship – the Galley – was being burnt in a spectacular climax to a torch-lit procession. In the twentieth century, Guizer Jarl or chief guiser, and his squad – a group of guisers dressed as Vikings – was introduced. Only men take part in the parade, although both men and women are involved in the preparations and other associated festivities. Since the 1950s, the festival has become larger, more efficient and expensive, and is enjoyed by both locals and visitors alike.

Guising was not unique to Shetland. It was often carried out at New Year and a procession of men and boys would go to each household in a community, knock on the walls, and walk round the houses in a sunwise direction. In return, they would be offered hospitality in the form of food and drink, usually bread, oatmeal and whisky. Galatian or Galoshans was a play that was traditionally performed by boys at Hogmanay. Again the church tried to prevent communities from participating in such cross-dressing rituals, and the church authorities recorded complaints about men dressing as women. Nowadays guising is usually confined to Hallowe'en.

As well as Imbolc or St Bride's Day, February also includes Candlemas on 2 February, which was the Feast of the Purification of the Virgin and a very important pre-Reformation Christian ritual; and St Blaise's Day on 3 February. Some local ball games were held on 2 February. The Jedburgh Boys Ba' Game is particularly well known. The Men's Game (and also the Hawick game) is held on Shrove Tuesday. In both games the Uppies and Doonies – membership of the teams depends where an individual was born in relationship to the mercat cross – compete for a ball that is decorated with ribbons. The game is played in the streets of the town and to the River Jed. A rather gruesome explanation for the origins of the game suggests that it commemorates a battle between locals and an invading English army – the ball represents the severed head of an unfortunate English soldier. Since there were numerous altercations between England and Scotland in the Border areas such an event may well have been likely. Alternatively, given the rivalry that is notorious between Border towns, it could be that the head represented an unfortunate visitor from a neighbouring town. Kirkwall on Orkney also celebrates a Ball Game, which is held on New Year's Day.

Another yearly ritual was known as the Borrowing Days. The last three days of March (before the change in the calendar) were called Borrowing Days, as it was claimed that March borrowed three days from April. At this time in some communities blood from animals would be mixed with oatmeal to make a pudding – the original black pudding. Although this became a kind of ritual, it should also be seen in the context of the agricultural year. Towards the end of March supply of foodstuffs would be declining – if not finished – apart from stores of meal. Blood-rich black pudding would be an efficient and cheap (the animal would not have to be slaughtered) nutritious meal.

Easter or Pasche was the most important Christian festival and, although it did not have a clear pre-Christian origin, nevertheless it did symbolise the passing of the old winter and the move into a new spring. The church, as opposed to the community, controlled many of the rituals that marked this time of year.

Other communal rituals incorporated both Christian and pre-Christian rituals. At Applecross, in Wester Ross, it was recorded that the locals ritually sacrificed a bull in order to bring good luck to the community. The ceremony took place annually on St Maelrubha's Day, 21 April (or 21 August) – Maelrubha was a saint from Ireland who had established a monastery here.

Shrines and Wells

One of the commonest means to remove illness was to use water. Although south-running water was important, as was water over which both the living and dead had passed, the most popular by far was well water. There were many wells throughout Scotland that developed a reputation for healing, or were associated with, a particular condition or ailment, such as skin conditions, infertility or whooping cough. The visit, and rituals, associated with these sources of water, or indeed any place of healing power, often took the form of a pilgrimage. Pilgrimage was a very common practice throughout medieval and early modern Scotland and Europe as a whole, and one that the pre-Reformation church embraced wholeheartedly. The sites themselves may have had pre-Christian origins or myths – for example it was believed that there was a guardian spirit at the Tobar Bial na Buaidh – well of the virtuous water and tree – near Benderloch. Offerings were left at a nearby tree in order to placate the spirit in return for assistance. Similarly it was believed that the water spirit in the Dow Loch in Dumfries and Galloway could cure several illnesses. Tobar Fuar, near Corgarff, was also believed to have a healing spirit. Wells and lochs, and water in general, may have been seen as a gateway to another realm. Perhaps water provided an interface between this world and another which was inhabited by fairies and other spirits.

The tradition of utilising miracles associated with places or people was a useful one for the pre-Reformation church, and many chapels were built on, or near, the sites of older pre-Christian holy wells. In order to provide comfort for troubled pilgrims, the church encouraged them to pray and leave offerings at the sites. The major pilgrimage sites in medieval Scotland were Tain, St Andrews, Dunfermline, Glasgow and Whithorn, but pilgrimages to local sites were just as popular. Routes of travel, including roads and bridges, were established with the encouragement of the church. The church also built chapels and hostels to provide for the needs of pilgrims. Pilgrimage was big business during the medieval period – perhaps one of the earliest form of tourist attractions – as travellers wearing their scallop-shaped badges or tokens, which indicated that they were on pilgrimage, were permitted to travel freely around the country and even abroad. Pilgrims also brought trade and custom to the communities near a pilgrimage site.

As the wells were assimilated into a Christian framework, they were dedicated to certain saints. It was claimed that they marked a place of birth, location of inhabitation, site of miracles, or area of missionary work of a saint, which passed into local and national tradition. Saints' relics were believed to have a range of powers, not least healing, so consequently any place with which the saint had some physical connection was also seen to be blessed.

Alternatively wells might be dedicated to one of the important figures in the Christian tradition, such as Mary or John. There were many wells dedicated to St Columba throughout Scotland, including ones in Argyll, Dumfries and Galloway, Highland and Lanarkshire. St Ninian, another native saint, also has a number of wells dedicated to him: at Arbroath, Dunnottar, Lamington, Nairn and Upper Barr. Saints Moluag, Maelrubha and Brendan also all had more than one site dedicated to them.

Local saints – those associated with a particular area – had wells, and later chapels built in close proximity, dedicated to them. St Mungo's or St Kentigern's Well in Glasgow had a nearby chapel that has been destroyed. There is an old healing well, dedicated to St Fergus, at Glamis. The later church, now Presbyterian, was built above the site of the well or spring. In an interesting recent development, which demonstrates the constant changes in society's attitudes, this area has recently been landscaped and visitors to the church are encouraged to make the short walk to the well, and even drink the water.

Perhaps the cynical might suggest that this is simply the local congregation trying to add to local visitor attractions – a carved Pictish stone, castle and folk museum are all nearby – but a more sympathetic view would be that they are taking a more open-minded view of their historical culture. Rather than condemning and criticising past customs as being pagan and superstitious, current attitudes are more accepting and understanding.

Water from Tobar a' Bhaistaidh at Portmahomack was used in baptisms. It was said that the well had been sanctified by St Rule. He drank water from here when he landed at Portmahomack on his way to St Andrews. The story goes he threw pieces of the Holy Cross into the water and blessed it. The water was used to baptise the eldest sons of the Earls of Cromartie. This tradition is claimed to have been started in the late seventeenth century by Kirsty Bheag, a local witch. This is another interesting mix of belief systems.

St Triduana's Well, at Restalrig in Edinburgh, had a collegiate church established nearby by James III in the 1460s. Triduana was not native to Restalrig, although she may have spent some years here; she also has associations with Rescobie in Angus, but may not even have been from Scotland. The collegiate church and chapel were both attacked by Reformers in the late sixteenth century and were ruinous until restored in 1836. Water from the well, or spring, issues from a stone under the floor in a separate hexagonal building (St Triduana's Well) by the present church, now dedicated to St Margaret. Although a parish in the Presbyterian Church of Scotland, requests to use the water are still received and supplied. The well was especially revered for eye conditions.

The Virgin Mary had numerous wells dedicated to her, including at Motherwell and Tobermory, as the names indicate. Motherwell indicating the well of the mother (of Christ) and Tobar from the Gaelic Tobar meaning well and Mory, meaning Mary. Other wells dedicated to Mary are recorded by the name Tobar Mhoire – Mary Well – or Lady Well. There was a Tobar

Mhoire near Alness and a Lady Well at St Mary's Chapel near Oldmeldrum. St Mary's Well, near Culloden, is a clootie well. The fame of some wells spread near and far, and St Mary's Well in Elgin was visited not just by people from the local district but by people from as far away as the Western Isles. There is also a St Mary's Well at Crosskirk in Caithness. St Mary's Well at Orton near Banff was still being visited by many people before the First World War, and the traditions was revived in the 1930s.

Aeneas Sylvius Piccolomini – who was later Pope Pious II – visited the well by St Mary's Church at Whitekirk, near North Berwick, in East Lothian in 1435. He did not visit the site because of its international reputation, although it had a widespread national following, but because of a much more personal reason. Pious had nearly been shipwrecked in a serious storm, and had vowed to walk to the first place of pilgrimage once he landed. His ship docked at Dunbar and Pious walked from there to Whitekirk. The pilgrimage site had a shrine built in 1309, after Agnes, Countess of Dunbar, claimed that she had been healed by water from a nearby well. It proved to be such a popular site that James I placed it under his protection, and had hostels built to provide shelter for pilgrims. It is recorded that as many as 15,000 people visited the shrine in 1413. Another notable international saint, John the Baptist, had wells dedicated to him near Dingwall and Laurencekirk.

The ritual of pilgrimage did not, however, sit well with the doctrine of the reformed church. The Protestant position rejected the power of saints – and relics – and claimed the age of miracles was past, but this did not stop people going on pilgrimage. In 1581, some years after the Reformation began, the parliament banned the practice in Scotland. It was not only going on a pilgrimage that was outlawed; the parliament banned a number of customs and rituals that were deemed to be unacceptable to the reformed faith. 'Forsmekill as pairt for want of doctrine and raritie of ministeris, and pairtlie throw the persuers inclicatioun of manis ingyne to superstitioun, the dregges of Idolatrie that remainis in divers pairtes of the realme be using of pilgramage to sum chappellis, wellis, croces and sic uther monumentis of Idolatrie. As also be observing of the festuall dayis of the santes, sumtyme namit their patronis in setting furth of bainfyris, singing of caroles ... at certane seasones of the yeir it is statut and ordainit be oure soverane lord, with advise of his thre estatis in this present parliament, that nane of his hines lieges use the saidis pilgramages or utheris the foirnamit superstitious and papisticall rytis'.

Despite passing such an act it was, however, very difficult to persuade local communities to abandon well-established, and popular, customs and festivals. During the late sixteenth and seventeenth centuries, the church fought an on-going battle with local congregations to try to stop them going to holy wells. Some presbyteries ordered ministers and elders to wait in hiding at wells, and other religious sites, in order to catch members of their congregations who continued to visit them. The enthusiasm with which this was carried out varied across the country; in some areas it would seem that local elders and ministers were less inclined to interfere. Notwithstanding the attempts at prevention by some local church authorities – the covering of wells with stones for example, which were then repeatedly removed – many communities were reluctant to change their habits. People were reprimanded for visiting the well and pool at St Wallach's at Dumeath, in the seventeenth century. In 1607 a group of people were ordered to make public repentance in front of the congregations at Airth and Bothkennar for going to Christ's Well near Stirling. It would appear that even in the eighteenth century visits to wells were still extremely popular, and Martin Martin, who travelled around the Western Isles in the late seventeenth and early eighteenth centuries, noted that people still visited Loch Siant Well, on the north-east coast of Trotternish on Skye. He recorded that people would visit the well, drink some of the water, walk around the well three times in a sunwise direction and leave a small votive offering. They visited the well in the hope of curing headaches and migraines, consumption, kidney or bladder stones and stitches. The offerings that were left included stones, rags, pins, coloured threads and coins.

Although offerings of coins and pebbles were common enough, the most widespread practice was leaving rags, threads or cloths. Many of these wells – known as clootie wells – were used into the twentieth century, and some are still being visited today. Munlochy Well, dedicated to St Curitan or Boniface, in the Black Isle, is still popular and the nearby trees are full of bits of clothing and rags, as well as the occasional written petition for assistance for a loved one. There is another clootie well – dedicated to St Bennet or Benedict – south of Cromarty, and also St Mary's Well at Culloden, and the trees around are decorated with brightly coloured cloth. St Queran's Well, at Islesteps near Dumfries, is still being visited and, along with cloths and ribbons tied to nearby trees, people have left rings and other bits of jewellery. It should be mentioned that it is believed that items should not be removed from a well as any illness or misfortune of the person who placed it there may then transfer to the person who took the item.

Nails and coins were hammered into an oak tree at St Maelrubha's Well on an island in Loch Maree in Wester Ross. Money was thrown into the water at a well at Dunnet and coloured stones left at a well on Gigha. Quartz pebbles were left at the Lix Well at Wester Lix near Killin, and women left pins and ribbons at St Conwall's Well at Huntingtower, near Perth. Offerings of cheese or food were, and are still, left at the Cheese Well on Minch Moor to ensure safe crossings (the old road now forms part of the Southern Upland Way).

Sometimes the wells were visited at particular times of the day or year. It was quite common to visit them on the Celtic quarter days – especially Beltane and Samhain. Midsummer was also another popular time, and some wells would be visited on their particular saint's day as the water was thought to be particularly efficacious at that time. As

Christianity dominated culture and belief, some of the visits moved from the Celtic quarter days to the Sunday nearest each one. The first Sunday in May became especially popular. Chapel Wells at Kirkmaiden, Craiguch or Tobar Chragag near Avoch, Jenny or Janet's Well at Portnockie were all visited on the first Sunday in May.

Other wells, such as St Serf's Well at Monzievaird at St Mary's Well at Orton near Banff, were visited on Lammas day, and the Braemou Well at Samhain or Hallowe'en. This well was claimed to provide protection from the evil eye. The Rose Well near Livingston, which was said to cure scrofula, was visited at sunrise on New Year's Day.

Some of the wells probably had a high mineral content, but this was generally not recognised or acknowledged until the eighteenth century. Certainly a number of them were chalybeate, or rich in iron, others were sulphurous and some were oily or tarry in appearance. These components may have explained the type of ailment or condition that was associated with the well, but others seem to have been simply natural springs with no chemical or mineral ingredient.

Some of the mineral wells were re-fashioned into spas in the eighteenth and nineteenth centuries. By this time, medical science had recognised the efficacy of some water treatments or hydropathy, either by immersion, ingestion, or topical application. The mineral well at St Ronan's at Innerleithen was used to treat a wide range of varying ailments: eye conditions, scurvy, and stomach complaints. The water at Strathpeffer is high in sulphur, and was very popular in the nineteenth century. The water here is smelly – due to its high sulphur content – and it is claimed that the Brahan Seer predicted, many decades before the nineteenth century, that, although it was thick and smelly with a crusty surface, people would eventually seek their health and pleasures from it. As with many of the Brahan Seer's prophecies, there is no way to prove this, but it makes a good story. Other sulphur wells were found at Letham and at Moffat. Both of these were also used to treat scurvy and other skin diseases, as well as kidney and bladder stones.

Women often visited iron rich chalybeate wells – the iron content may well have proved useful if they were anaemic. The Hart Fell Spa near Moffat was visited by women, although other chalybeate wells, such as the ones at Pannanich, near Ballater and the Virtue Well near Airdrie, were used to treat scrofula – or lymphatic tuberculosis – and skin diseases. The Merkland Well at Lochrutton was also iron-rich, but it was used to treat stomach and nervous complaints (the two might have been related) and ague, which was a form of malaria-like fever.

Some wells were associated with a specific type of illness or complaint; others appear to have been used to treat everything and anything. The Lady Well near Airth and the well associated with the Lady of Loretto in Musselburgh were popular pilgrimage sites because it was believed they could cure a variety of general conditions. The Physick Well at Turriff was also a general cure-all, although it was a chalybeate well. Water from St Michael's Well in Linlithgow, St Ninian's (or St Ringan's) in Stirling, St Peter's in Houston, and St Thenew's (or St Enoch's) in Glasgow was used for general medicinal purposes. The spring or well known as Tobar nam Buaidh or well of virtues or special powers, which is on St Kilda, was another cure-all well.

Sometimes it was not just a drink or an application of the water that was required: people bathed in the water at St Wallach's well at Dumeath, and sickly children were plunged at dawn into the cold water at the Claggan Well in Kenmore. Perhaps the cold water shocked them into recovering!

Mental illness

A similar use of water is seen in the rituals associated with St Fillan at Strathfillan and St Maelrubha on an island in Loch Maree – although these were specifically for people with mental or emotional conditions. In 1772 Thomas Pennant noted that

St Maelrubha's Well was used in 'cases of lunacy'. It was still being used to treat mental illness in the nineteenth century. In 1850 a local boy became disturbed. His friends and family took the boy to the island where he was immersed in the water. He was then tied to the back of the boat and towed three times round the island. It was not recorded how often this treatment worked but on this occasion, sadly, the boy was not cured.

St Fillan's Pool was also used to treat insanity. The patients were immersed in the pool, then carried to the nearby chapel. There they lay down, were tied with ropes and had the chapel bell (which was believed to have curative powers in its own right) placed over their head. They would be left on their own overnight and in the morning if they were found untied then it was thought they might be cured. If they were still secured by the ropes, then any chance of recovery was said to be unlikely.

People who were emotionally disturbed were also left tied at Eoropie on Lewis. This may have been at St Ronan's Chapel or Well, near St Moluag's Church. Another version reported that the insane person was walked seven times round the ruins of an older chapel, or the present St Moluag's Church, and then sprinkled with some of the water from the well, before they were left alone overnight. In another similar case, four men from the Stirling area secured an emotionally disturbed woman at a well at Struthill and left her alone overnight. In their testimony, they claimed that the ropes were loosened the next morning, but she remained in the same state. They carried out the same ritual a second time and on the second morning she had regained her senses. The woman gave a confession to the church authorities about what had happened and claimed that she had recovered. The four men were reprimanded. The well may have been St Patrick's Well, near Stirling, which, despite having been ordered to be destroyed in the seventeenth century, was still being used to treat madness in the eighteenth century.

Eye Conditions

Several wells dedicated to St John were thought to be helpful in the treatment of eye disease. These were found at Moffat, Falkland and Inverkeithing. The well at Falkland was on land owned by the Order of the Knights Templar and the one at Inverkeithing by the Knights of St John. The water at the well of St Triduana at Restalrig was believed to cure blindness and other eye problems. The site has already been discussed but the story associated with St Triduana, although it is not unique to Scotland, explains the connection between Triduana and eyes. It was claimed that Triduana (also known as Tredwell and Trodwin) was a Pictish princess, who had founded a chapel at Rescobie. She had converted to Christianity and wanted to dedicate her life to Christ. Nechtan, a prince from another tribe, who had not converted, desired her but she refused his advances. Nechtan was especially taken with her beautiful eyes, and Triduana climbed a thorn tree to escape his advances. She is then said to have plucked out her eyes and thrown them to him, skewered on a thorn. Another version claimed that rather than being a local Pictish princess, Triduana was Greek and had arrived in Scotland with Rule – later St Rule. There are parallel stories from Ireland and the Continent so the truth of the Scottish version is questionable.

Tobar na Suil – well of the eye – on the island of Luing, off the west coast of Argyll, was also used to treat eye troubles. The spring here flows into a small hollow, which was thought to resemble an eyeball and because of this physical resemblance it was claimed the water was useful for eye problems.

St Ronan's Well at Innerleithen was thought to cure eye disease, as did the water from St Medana's or Chapel Wells at Kirkmaiden. There were three different sized wells here, and traditionally they were visited on the first Sunday in May, before sunrise. The sufferer would be immersed first in the largest pool, then the middle pool and finally water from the smallest one would be used to bathe the eyes. Finally, an offering was left at the well. Medana (she is also known as Modwenna,

Medina or Medan) has a similar story to Triduana's associated with her. She was a pursued by an amorous admirer, and took refuge on a rock. When he would not desist, she plucked out her own eyes and threw them at her would-be lover. Presumably, this put him off. When she returned to the shore, she asked for water to clean the blood from her face. A spring suddenly burst forth, and using the water her eyes were restored.

Rheumatism

St Fillan was associated with a number of sites in Perthshire and a number of different problems, including insanity, infertility and rheumatism – they do not seem to have any connection. St Fillan's Well, at Loch Earn, was visited both by women suffering from infertility and people who had rheumatism. St Fillan's Chair and Well at Dunfillan were visited at Beltane and Lammas: the chair was believed to cure rheumatism.

Beauty and Fertility

The connection between well water and conception are international. Wells were visited to aid conception in countries including Greece, India, China, Africa and Israel. Some of these wells – if Christianised – were dedicated to Mary, Our Lady or the Holy Virgin, but there were other saint's wells that were also thought to provide assistance with fertility. St Fillan's has already been covered. St Bride's Well, at Corgarff, would be visited by women on the night before they were to be married, and they would wash their feet and upper body in the water. A votive offering of bread and cheese would be left, and it was claimed that this ritual would ensure a healthy and fertile marriage. The Malsach Well at Knockandy Hill was believed to restore fertility to women who were having difficulty conceiving again.

St Anthony's Well, in Holyrood Park in Edinburgh, was believed to help improve the appearance and their skin: people would wash their faces in water from the well on 1 May or Beltane day. This tradition continued into later years, well after the church had condemned the use of well water, but latterly dew was substituted for well water.

Allergic Diseases: Asthma and Skin Conditions
A number of wells were believed to help with either or both of these conditions. St Aidan's Wells, located at Balmerino, Cambusnethan, Fearn and Menmuir, were associated with both ailments. The wells at Menmuir and Cambusnethan were also known as St Iten's Wells.

Water from St Catherine's Balm Well at Liberton in Edinburgh, was used to treat skin problems, including eczema. The balm well at Liberton was visited by James IV and refurbished by his great-grandson James VI. In 1617 James VI ordered the building of steps and stones so that there would be easier access to the well. The water contains a tarry substance, which would account for its usefulness in treating inflamed or irritated skin. Another legend claimed that the well sprang from a drop of holy oil that was being transported from the Holy Land to Queen (later Saint) Margaret. It is now in the grounds of the Balmwell, which is a restaurant. Some accounts have the name Liberton being derived from Lepers' Town, which may relate to the use of the well for skin diseases, and even leprosy. The term 'ton', however, usually refers to a farm, and it is not clear if there was ever a leper colony here.

Scurvy was treated using water from the Crystal Well at Whittinghame. There were other St Catherine's Wells at Alva, Banff, Fyvie and Watten. It is not known if they were also used to treat skin disease. St Ronan's Well at Innerleithen, which has already been mentioned, was said to help treat skin conditions such as that caused by scurvy.

St Bride's Well near Port-na-Craig was claimed to cure respiratory conditions. Pins and coins were dropped into the water, and rags were tied to nearby bushes.

Whooping Cough

Whooping cough, or pertussis, appears to have been quite a common complaint, judging by the range of wells that were specifically used to treat it. Kinkhost or chincough were Scottish terms for the disease and there were a number of wells given this name. A well at Kingarth near Comrie was called the Kinkhost Well. There was a Chincough Well near Glasserton, which was also dedicated to St Medana. Tobar nan Dileag, or well of the drips, near Tillichuil, was used to treat children with whooping cough. There were two wells at Garth Castle near Fortingall. One was called Fuaran a' Gruarach – spring of the measles – and the other, Fuaran a' Druibh Chasad – spring of the cough – and they were still being used in the late nineteenth century. Water from St Thomas's Well, near Crieff, was also used to treat measles and coughs. St Mary's Well at Orton was also used for whooping cough, as well as eye diseases and rheumatism.

Toothache

A common complaint in the early modern period was toothache. In the absence of dentists, or alternatively blacksmiths, sufferers would turn to a number of remedies, some of which will be covered in the following sections, but well water was also popular. The Fuaran Fionntag – or well of virtue – near Duthil was believed to relieve the pain. There were also wells at Craig Castle near Rhynie and at Tobar Chuithairigh (also known as Tobar an Deideidh or well of the toothache) on North Uist, which were used to treat toothache. The well at Craig Castle is also believed to be a wishing well – perhaps the toothache was wished away rather than cured. Other wells that were specifically used to treat toothache were located at Kenmore and Glentruim.

Good Luck Wells

Even today when people visit wells it is quite common to drop a coin or two into them and make a wish – perhaps not for any specific reason but more for general good luck or protection. There are many such general good luck wells around Scotland. The Braemou Well was thought to provide protection from the evil eye. Water from St Corbett's Well near Stirling was drunk in the hope that it would bring good luck and long life

Although most of the population was involved in working on the land, a number of communities were reliant on the sea to provide food, fuel, transport and an income. Some good luck wells were believed to ensure favourable winds for those about to embark on a journey or fishing trip. Tobar na Cille or St Brendan's Well, on St Kilda, was used by local people to bring a good wind when they set out on a journey to Harris. Tobar nan Gaeth Deas, or well of the south wind, is located on Colonsay, and was visited by fishermen and other sailors. Votive offerings were left in the belief that a good south wind would result. On Gigha, water from the Tobar a' Beathaig would be thrown into the sea in order to ensure a favourable wind.

Animal disease

Since life was dependent on agriculture, the health of animals was very important. Like dentists, vets were not available and people resorted to their own experience or local knowledge to cure their beasts. A number of wells were not only used to treat humans, but were also believed to cure animals. Some appear to have been used to treat only animals. The Slot Well, Barskeoch Hill neat Buittle, was used to treat connoch or cattle plague. Many tethers and other pieces of animal equipment were left behind. Ladycross or Pennyglen's Cross Well was said to specifically cure muirill or moorill, also known as red water. This was an infection that caused cattle to have red or bloody urine.

Water from the Malsach Well at Knockandy Hill was used to treat both humans and animals.

AMULETS AND TALISMANS

A mulets and talismans were usually used as protective or apotropaic devices. In other words, they were used before a problem had developed. On occasion, however, they were also used to cure. Most amulets were worn, rather than applied or ingested, although some were tied or placed in a room rather than worn on the body. What was important was that they were near to the person or animal. The protective power of amulets may have been symbolic, rather than chemical, as there may have been a strong psychological factor in their use, in that they provided emotional security for the wearer or user. This would only be true for humans – whether or not animals were aware of the psychological benefits is perhaps a moot point, but presumably their owners were the ones who needed reassured.

Amulets and talismans could take various forms. An apotropaic amulet usually took the form of a trinket or some small piece of jewellery, which was worn as protection from the evil eye. A talisman was some small stone or paper, often inscribed or carved with words or letters, which also protected the wearer from harm. It was thought that the power of these talismans came from the inscriptions. Jewellery itself was relatively rare but metals, precious or semi-precious gems, wood, beans, stones and other natural produce were all used for healing or protective purposes. Amulets could also be made of herbs or plants.

Gold was a precious metal and universally prized for its monetary value, but at the same time had numerous beliefs associated with its magical power. One of its most frequent uses was in treating eye conditions. Wedding rings were rubbed over a stye in order to help the condition. Rubbing the ears with gold was also thought to help eye problems. As a more general good luck charm, it was also thought that rubbing gold over the eyes of those who did not have styes would bring them good fortune – unless of course it had just been rubbed over a stye, in which case the outcome may have been a spread of the disease. Drinking water that had been poured over gold was also claimed to have curative value.

Gold leaf was also used in medicines that were prescribed in the early-modern period. Some tablets or capsules were covered with gold. Even a recipe for cordial water used gold leaf amongst no less that eighty ingredients, which also included coral, pearl, and amber.

Silver was also used in a number of ways to protect against harm or to cure ailments. Silver was associated with the moon, and therefore was seen to have connection with witchcraft and other demonic powers. Turning over a silver coin in the pocket at the first sight of a new moon was believed to bring good luck and protection. Silver – either as a brooch, pin or coin – attached to, or placed near, a baby would protect it from witches and also fairies. A silver coin or other form around the neck was said to help cure scrofula.

Silver was also used to mount other stones or charms, notably crystal and elfshot, and the resultant amulet may well have had a doubling of its protective powers. Elfshot was the name given to prehistoric arrowheads. These were often uncovered during ploughing and, before later archaeology identified them as prehistoric, agricultural communities found another explanation for them. It was thought that these unusual objects – clearly not made by their contemporaries – were made by the fairies or elves. The darts were then used to harm livestock – usually cattle – by being thrown at the animals by the fairies. Any sudden death or episode of illness was blamed on the interference of evil powers, and sick animals were often said to have been elfshot. As a means of redress, ownership of one of these elfshots could also provide the means to protect or cure. Some of them were mounted in silver, and used as an amulet to protect against future harm or damage.

Silver bullets were also believed to be able to kill demons or the un-dead. It was claimed by his enemies that John

Graham of Claverhouse – Viscount Dundee – who was also known as Bonnie Dundee and Bloody Clavers, depending on which side people were, could only be killed by a silver bullet. Dundee was shot and killed at the Battle of Killiecrankie during the 1689 Jacobite Rising, but it is not recorded if it was a silver bullet that delivered the fatal wound. Vampires were also thought to be vulnerable to silver bullets, but there are few vampire stories from Scotland, although a visit to Slains Castle, now a ruin, in the north-east of Scotland is thought to have inspired Bram Stoker to write his novel about Dracula. There is vampire story connected with Melrose Abbey. The spirit of a monk was reputed to haunt the cloister area. It was said that, despite his vows of poverty and obedience, he had lived a life of sin and debauchery, and became a vampire. He would venture out at night and return to his grave at dawn. Apparently he attacked the abbess of the nearby convent. He was finally defeated, not with a silver bullet however, but by a fellow monk who beheaded him with an axe, although presumably the axe head would have been made of iron, another powerful metal.

Iron is particularly associated with fire. It has been used by man for centuries and, due to its remarkable properties, was regarded as one of the most powerful of the metals. Cross-culturally it was seen to have apotropaic powers and was capable of warding off evil powers. Because of their work with fire and molten metals, blacksmiths were believed to have special skills and knowledge. Smiths made weaponry and armour, as well as agricultural implements and tools, and so were vital members of a community or clan, and were highly respected. There was also an association with the Celtic god of smiths Gobniu, who had mystical healing powers, and smiths were often consulted about healing advice.

Witches and fairies were not able to cross iron. Iron horseshoes or nails were often secreted about the bed or room when a woman was in childbirth, as this was a very vulnerable time for both mother and child. A piece of iron at a threshold was believed to prevent evil spirits, or their power, crossing into a house, which is why horseshoes were often attached above a doorway. Iron nails had the same effect.

Iron nails were also believed to cure toothache in a number of ways. They could be hammered into a stone. Touching the part of the body that was diseased, then hammering the nail into a tree, reflected a similar belief. A nail taken from a coffin could be also placed under the affected tooth, and biting on a piece of iron the day before Easter was said to prevent toothache for the rest of the year. It was thought that nails laid on the chests of corpses before burial would prevent their spirits coming back to haunt their relatives. Passing a hot iron over the spine of the afflicted person was used as a treatment for jaundice. Plunging a red-hot poker into a churn would help the butter form, and prevent witches stealing the goodness of the milk.

The use of lead as a diagnostic tool has already been covered but after the 'lead was cast', that is poured into water, the congealed piece was often worn over the patient's heart, as an amulet, in the belief that it would counteract any harm.

Amber beads, or 'lammer' as they were known in Scotland, were regarded as lucky and had several beliefs associated with them. According to legend, they were the result of the tears of the sisters of the Greek hero Meleager, and pieces of amber had been worn as amulets since classical times. Strings of amber beads were worn as protection against eye diseases, which may reflect this ancient myth. It was thought that amber beads protected children, particularly against witchcraft and nightmares. In some countries, amber was also thought to cure asthma and whooping cough, although this was not recorded in Scotland.

Molluka (or molucca) beans were the seeds of the *Ipomaca Tuberosa* and *Guildandia Bonduc*, which originated in the West Indies. They were washed up on the western shores of Scotland, particularly on the Western Isles, because of the Gulf Stream. In Gaelic they were called Cno Mhoire but they were also known as Virgin Mary's Nut or St Mary's Nut, and would occasionally be mounted in silver. If the natural marks on the bean overlapped in the shape of a cross they were regarded as being especially powerful, and the white ones were supposed to turn black if the wearer was threatened by witchcraft or some form of harm.

The beans were worn as amulets around the neck, and had a number of purposes. They were believed to prevent drowning; and they helped with childbirth. The bean would be held in the right hand of the woman who was in labour and she would repeat the Hail Mary three times. The midwife would then take the bean and make the sign of the cross over the woman. Molluka beans were also used in animal husbandry, particularly dairy work. If a cow gave blood-streaked milk, it was believed that the milk had been stolen by witchcraft. To counteract the spell, a bean would be placed into the milking pail and the blood-streaked milk would turn the bean brown. The next time the cow was milked, the same bean would be placed in the pail but this time the milk would be clear.

Pieces of wood, roots and herbs were also used as amulets. Pieces of rowan would be tied to animals' tails to ward off any harmful spirits. Often the rowan was combined with red thread as it was said that 'Rowan tree and red thread, gar the witches tyne their speed'. James VI noted that rowan and other types of herbs were tied to the hair and tails of animals to protect them from the evil eye. People would also sometimes carry small twigs of rowan or put one in their hats for good luck. It was also thought that carrying a bit of a rowan twig would prevent rheumatism.

The root of the groundsel was used to protect milk from being stolen or lost. It was also used to treat bruises and boils. Germander speedwell was believed to have protective properties, and its seeds were included in amulets to be worn around the neck by those who were preparing to go into battle. Potato was also used as form of vegetable amulet. In the nineteenth century, it was commonly held that carrying a piece of potato in the pocket was a certain cure for rheumatism – although, given that there were so many other cures for this condition, it would seem that none of them were that certain.

Amulets could also come in a number of other forms. Red thread was believed to have protective properties. It was often tied around the wrists of small children to protect them from witches and the evil eye. On the other hand, red silk was used to prevent or cure rheumatism. These days copper bands are sold as remedies against rheumatic pains – perhaps red silk might be worth trying.

Sulphur was used to treat cramp in Aberdeenshire and Fife. In Fife a piece of sulphur would be sewn into a garter and worn around the leg. On other occasions pieces of sulphur were placed under the oxter, or armpit, or under the pillow.

Words were very important in a number of magical healing rituals. In many cases they would be used in the form of an incantation or verbal formula. There were three basic types: prayers, blessings, and adjurations. Prayers took the form of requests to God, Jesus, Mary or a particular saint; blessings were wishes and addressed to the sufferers; and adjurations were commands to the sickness (or more accurately the demonic power causing the sickness) to depart. Very often the words were used along with a specific ritual or performance – perhaps making the sign of the cross or winding threads round the afflicted part.

Another way to use words was to write them down – on some occasions it was believed that the written kind was more effective than spoken charms. Some contained series of letters written in a particular order. Others contained words that were usually in the form of a prayer or contained extracts from the Bible – in Gaelic this was known as soisgeul – and would often be sealed before being given to the recipient. Talismans were used throughout medieval Europe, and similar scriptural talismans or phylacteries were also used in Greek, Roman and Jewish traditions.

Very often those receiving the talisman could not read the words themselves. Latin would have been difficult to read for most, and, for Gaelic-speaking communities, English would have been just as problematic. Being in an unfamiliar language may have added to the perceived magical power of the words. It also added to the power of the healer – anyone who had knowledge of reading and writing and the Scriptures would have been seen as very powerful.

Talismans were usually worn round the neck, round the arm, or in a shoe. They were different from amulets, which were usually used to provide general protection. Although there were talismans to protect against fire, poison and attack, and others to bring good luck, many were used to treat or cure a pre-existing condition. They were worn as long as possible until they fell off or rotted. One explanation was that as the talisman deteriorated, so did the ailment. They were not to be interfered with or removed too soon, or they would not be effective. The recipient should not look at or read the words, or again their power would be lost

A well-known example of a healing talisman was one for toothache. It was used throughout mainland Scotland, and both in the Western and Northern Isles. The basic formula for the toothache repeated a story attributed to St Peter, based on the following version. Peter the Apostle sat on a stone weeping. Jesus came by and asked, 'What aileth thee?' 'Toothache my Lord,' replied Peter. 'Rise up and he who believeth in me and my name shall be cured of the toothache.' The words were written on a piece of paper, which was then folded a specific number of times then worn around the neck. The paper was not to be opened and looked at or removed or it would not work.

Threads or ribbons were another form of amulet or talisman. Although they did not involve written words they did, however, often involve the use of the spoken word. A spoken charm would usually be uttered as they were wrapped around the affected part of the body. Often a specific number of threads were used or they were to be of a particular colour. They would be wrapped around the patient a specific number of times and sometimes involved the tying of a special number of knots. Green thread was wound round an injury, and two black silk threads were wound round the body as a cure for scrofula.

The use of knots was recorded in a number of ways. One was the link between knots and the wind, which has a classical background. Winds could be purchased by sailors, which were contained in a bag or a cloth. A tale describes how some men wanted to get back to Uist from Lewis, but they were prevented from doing so by bad weather. An old woman approached the men and said she could help them in return for some snuff. The men agreed, and she gave them a thread with three knots in it. She told them they would get off the next day, but if the wind was not strong enough then the skipper could untie one of the knots. If that did not work, he could untie the second knot, but on no account was he to untie the third one. The men set off with a gentle wind, but needless to say they were soon dissatisfied and desired a stronger wind. The first knot was untied and the wind got stronger. The men remained impatient and soon untied the second knot. Once again the wind grew stronger and they were soon in sight of their home. Ignoring the words of the old woman, they decided to untie the final knot. Some versions have the boat returned to its original starting point, but in others it sank and the crew were drowned.

Knots were also associated with sex and childbirth. Although relatively rare in Scottish witchcraft material, a belief about witches' power that was common throughout Europe was that a witch could cause impotence if she tied a knot in a handkerchief. In Scotland, knots feature in folk beliefs about childbirth and are often associated with delayed or difficult childbirth. During labour, a woman's hair would be loosened and combed, and windows and locks opened to ensure a speedy and easy birth.

Knots were also used to cure warts, although in this case they were used in a slightly different way. A piece of string would be rubbed over the warts, and then knots were tied in the string corresponding to the number of warts. The string would then be buried and as it rotted the warts would improve. Another similar use involved wrapping a thread three times around a finger, then dropping the thread on the ground, in order to transfer the wart to whoever picked it up.

A cure for sprains that was used in Shetland involved the tying of black woollen thread, which had nine knots in it, around the injured limb. At the same time the following verse would be spoken: 'The Lord rade and the foal slade; He lighted and he righted, Let joint to joint, bone to bone, And sinew to sinew heal, In the Holy Ghost's name.'

A similar charm was known as the charm of the thread or eolas an t-snaithein, although it did not use knots. Three threads, one each of red, white, and black (or blue) were wrapped about the affected part of the body, and a prayer was uttered at the same time. Red threads, wound round the neck, were used as a charm to expel evil spirits from the head.

Another Shetland cure used a handful of three types of straw. Barley, Scots oats, and Shetland oats, made into the shape of a cross, were used to treat a child that had been scalded or burnt. The child's bed or cradle would be touched with the cross – first the underside, then the head. It would then be taken to the fire, and the healer would say a prayer, before using the cross to touch the burns.

STONES

Stones of various size and shape were also believed to have special or magical powers. They were thought to have protective, curative and symbolic powers because of their size, shape, appearance, location and history.

Large stones including stone settings – circle and other groupings – and single standing stones are believed to have been sacred sites from earliest times. Callanish on Lewis is one of the most complex and impressive. There are many other settings throughout Scotland, including the Hill o' Many Stanes in Caithness, Clava Cairns near Inverness, Machrie Moor on Arran, and the Ring of Brodgar and Stones of Stenness on Orkney. Stone circles and settings are not unique to Scotland, and there are also spectacular examples at Stonehenge and Avebury in England and Carnac in France.

Many of these were constructed during the Neolithic and early Bronze Age, and are located in spectacular settings. They still dominate the landscape even today. It is likely that they had some particular purpose, and may have been meeting places for rituals and ceremonies. There is quite a lot of variation in size and shape – often due to local topography and geology. Astronomical function has been suggested for some stone circles. Callanish has been interpreted as a lunar observatory, and Kintraw, north of Kilmartin in Argyll, can be shown to mark the Paps of Jura at the winter solstice. Archaeological evidence has revealed that ritual feasting may have occurred at some of the sites; bones from sheep and cattle have been found at the Stones of Stenness. Those structures that contain burial cairns within their boundaries suggest also suggest that the locations and stones were spiritually important to communities over many generations and thousands of years.

Over the centuries legends and explanations about the stone settings have been incorporated into local folklore. A stone at Strontoiller near Oban was said to commemorate the burial of the Irish hero Diarmid, and the ones at Lundin Links in Fife were claimed to mark the graves of Viking warriors defeated by Macbeth. Later generations then incorporated them into their customs and beliefs. Some stones were used for seasonal ceremonies and ritual observances, including Midsummer and New Year. Others were used for sealing contracts, including marriage or handfasting ceremonies, for tests of veracity, and for healing.

Some large stones that were claimed to have a specific shape were thought to cure particular ailments. Stones shaped like teeth were used to relieve the pain of toothache; those that were shaped like chairs were thought to help fertility and childbirth, as well as rheumatism. Stones with holes were also used to help with pregnancy and childbirth – women passed through them as a re-enactment of a birth. Holed stones were also used to treat chest complaints including asthma and consumption.

Holed stones were also used in other ways. Sometimes they were visited on a particular day or festival, particularly Beltane or New Year. On Orkney, young couples who intended to live together as husband and wife without being wed visited the Stone of Odin, which was part of the Stones of Stenness. The ceremony was known as handfasting, which was an arrangement between the man and woman that they would live together for a year and a day. The ceremony did not need the permission or involvement of a religious official, but the rest of the community acknowledged the relationship. In many respects this was a very sensible arrangement: if the couple did not wish to stay together for any reason – lack of children or incompatibility – they could separate without any stigma. Any child conceived during that year would not be regarded as illegitimate. Theoretically, the couple should then have had an official religious ceremony, but it is likely that many did not.

The couple would carry out a ritualised ceremony, first kneeling, walking and praying, and finally clasping their hands through the hole. Offerings of bread and cheese or rags would be left at the stone. According to tradition, if the couple later chose to divorce they could do this by leaving Stenness Church by different doors.

This ritual of handfasting, or plighting of their troth, continued into the nineteenth century when it was halted rather abruptly by the tenant farmer. Captain MacKay did not like the large numbers of people who were traipsing over his land, and decided to smash the stones and destroy the circle. He broke the Stone of Odin, but the tradition continued despite the absence of the hole. Only four of the original twelve Stones of Stenness survived.

The Hole Stone at Crouse was also used for handfasting, as was another Hole Stone at Dalry. Other holed stones were also used for marriage contracts or handfasting. The Dagon Stone at Darvel had a slightly different tradition, although it was also related to marriage. Dagon was a Philistine god (half-man, half-fish who was thought to ensure fertility); however, the word dagone also means villain in Scots, and this may have been a sanctuary stone. Newly married couples would walk round the stone in order to ensure good luck and fortune in their marriage. This was also done at Granny Kempock Stone at Kempock Point at Gourock. This is a six-foot-tall stone and, traditionally, couples and fishermen would walk round it seven times, carrying a basket of sand. It was believed that this would bring good winds and catches for the fishermen and success and happiness for the newly weds. In 1662 Mary Lawmont (or Lamont) was accused, with other women, of attempting to throw the Kempock Stone into the Clyde as part of a charge of witchcraft. Some of the women confessed that they intended to destroy boats and ships by this act. The women were not successful, and were most likely executed.

Some other ceremonies were also carried out at holed stones, including oaths and contracts. The Truth or Priest's Stone at Trumpan Church on Skye was used to discover the truthfulness of an individual. The person would be blindfolded, and had to insert their index finger into a specific hole in order to prove that they were telling the truth. If they did not manage to locate the hole, it was thought that they were lying. There were also stones on Iona – the Black Stones – which were said to change colour if someone lied while they were taking an oath.

A number of stones were believed to bring good luck, although sometimes only in return for offerings. There were several stones that were known as Clach na h-Iobairte or Stone of the Offering. It was believed that spirits of the stones could be enticed to offer assistance in return for offerings. A stone near Fortingall, overlooking Loch Rannoch, and another at Bridge of Tilt, were thought to bring good luck.

Quite often the offerings were of some foodstuff, particularly milk. Some of the stones were named after gruagach – supernatural beings who watched over cattle and dairy work – and offerings of milk were left at these stones in return for good harvests and other agricultural benefits. Offerings of milk were left at the Clach na Gruagach on Colonsay. Marks on the stone were said to have been caused by ropes that were used to tie the gruagach to it. Another stone, the Brownie Stone, on North Uist, would be visited by people from the local community on Sundays, who would also leave offerings of milk.

At Fyvie there was a stone referred to as the Shargar Stone. It was part of a ruined church, and consisted of one stone supported on top of two others. Sickly or weak children were passed through the space as it was thought that this would help the child recover. In Scots shargar means a puny or weak person.

Water that had gathered on tombstones was used to treat whooping cough or kinkhost. Sufferers from consumption would visit the Clach Thuill or Holed Stone at Crossapol on Coll. There is also a Clach Thuill on Oronsay and at Port Appin. As well as passing through or under the hole, the ritual often involved the use of prayer and offerings.

A granite rock on top of a hill near Glenavon called Clach-bhan or Stone of the Woman was shaped like a chair. When a pregnant woman was near her delivery date she would sit on the hollow of the stone as it was claimed this would ease her labour. Unmarried women also used the stone. They would visit the stone in the belief that it would help them find a suitable husband. Similarly, St Margaret's Stone at Pitreavie near Dunfermline, would also be visited by those wishing to conceive and have a successful birth. It was associated with St Margaret of Scotland, who had eight successful births: six sons (four of them Kings of Scots) and two daughters, one who went on to be Queen of England. St Margaret's Sark, or shirt, was also used by several queens to ensure a successful birth. Margaret also used a cave at Dunfermline as her retreat: it can still be visited, although it now lies under a car park.

St Fillan's Chair, at Dunfillan, is also shaped liked a chair. Sufferers from rheumatism would sit on the stone, then they were dragged down the hillside on their backs. This sounds like quite a painful experience, and the discomfort of the journey might take the patient's mind off their rheumatism. There is evidence, however, of other treatments that had a similar strategy. A number recommended the application of irritants (or counter-irritants) – these included things like nettles or heat – which increased local irritation and may have stimulated the production of endorphins (naturally occurring pain-relieving agents).

Toothache appears to have been a common complaint – as it still is today – and there were a number of different treatments used to cure the trouble. One of these included the use of large stones into which nails or pins were hammered. Although it is not entirely clear what was done, it may have been that hair or nail trimmings from the affected person were nailed into the stone and as they rotted away the pain from the tooth would fade. A stone near Port Charlotte on Islay and one at Brackley in Argyll were used in this way. The stone at Brackley was known as Carraig na Talaidh or Soothing Rock. Oak trees were also used in a similar fashion.

Smaller stones such as crystals and other types of quartz were believed to be especially powerful. They were thought to have magical healing and protective powers. Large crystals were often the property of an individual family, and they were often mounted in elaborate silver settings. Numerous legends about the miraculous powers of these objects developed, and many of the crystals were passed down through many generations. It was not only the family or those related to them who would seek to use them. Sometimes tenants, or even people from other communities, would request permission to use the healing power of the crystals.

The Campbells of Glenlyon owned the Clach Bhuaidh or Stone of Virtue. It was used to cure illness in both humans and animals. The Ballochyle Brooch, a crystal set in silver, now held at the Museum of Scotland, was also the property of a branch of the Campbell family. It was used to cure animals and humans, and was dipped in water. The water was then used to cure the patient by being sprinkled over them. The crystal had transferred its power to the water, and the water then contained the magical-healing power.

The Clach Dearg or Red Stone of Ardvorlich is also held by the Museum of Scotland. Despite its name, it is a crystal mounted in silver. It was dipped in water and the water was then used to bless the affected person. Sometimes it was rubbed over the affected areas. The MacDonnells of Keppoch held the Keppoch Stone. It was dipped into a spring known as St Brigid's Well, in Lochaber, and a prayer was said over the water.

The Lee Penny was used in the same way. It is a small red stone, set in silver, and owned by the Lockhart family. The stone was dipped in water three times and swirled around in a sunwise direction. The church investigated its use in the seventeenth century. This was during the years of investigation and prosecution of witchcraft and other 'sacrilegious' practices:

even the laird of Lockhart was not above investigation by the authorities. It was decided that since he had not used words as a prayer or incantation during the ritual the practice was acceptable. Requests would be made to the Lockhart family for water to cure humans and animals, usually cattle. Its reputation was quite widespread: the town council of Newcastle was said to have asked to use the amulet during an outbreak of plague in 1645.

Some small stones were used to cure specific ailments. Small holed stones – known as Serpent Stones or Adder Stones – were believed to have the power to cure snakebites. In Gaelic they are known as Glaine Nathrach or serpent glass, and have been identified as being prehistoric or Iron Age spindle whorls. Like the prehistoric arrowheads that were thought to be elf arrows or elfshot, these ancient artefacts were believed to be mysterious and have extraordinary powers. They were used to cure snakebites in cattle, but, given the overall lack of poisonous snakes in Scotland, it is more likely they were used to treat other symptoms that were claimed to be snakebites. Often these symptoms included skin peeling or flaking. Red thread was put through the hole, the stone was then dipped in water, which was then used to bathe or wash the afflicted part, and sometimes also given as a drink.

Other small stones, possibly fossils, were also used to treat a number of other conditions. Ones called snail stones, which were small glass beads, were used to cure sore eyes. There were others called cock's knee-stones and frog stones: the latter were used to staunch bleeding. They were all used in the same way: dipped in water to transfer the healing power to the water, or were rubbed over the affected area. St Fillan used eight different healing stones, each shaped like a different part of the head or body. These stones are now housed in the Breadalbane Folklore Centre in Killin by the Falls of Dochart.

Small stones called Hectic Stones or *Lapus Hecticus*, which were small pieces of rose or white quartz, were thought to cure fever or rheumatism. The white ones were said to have belonged to fairies. Some accounts say that the stones were put into boiling water; others state that the stones were heated first, and then put into water to cool. Once the water had cooled, it was used to wash the affected areas, particularly the arms and legs in the case of rheumatism. The water could also be drunk to relieve outbreaks of fever. According to Martin Martin, who described their use in the seventeenth century, they were also used to treat consumption. In this case either milk or water could be used

The Ball Mo-Luidhe or Molingus Globe was used on Arran. It was a green stone about the size of a goose egg, and was used to treat those suffering from a stitch (probably more than just a transitory pain). It was placed in the bed beside the sufferer in the hope that the disease would transfer to the stone; if the patient was not going to recover then the stone would remove itself of its own accord. The stone was held by the Mackintoshes, who kept it for the MacDonalds. It was used during the taking of ceremonial oaths, and was also claimed to have protective powers when it was thrown at enemy forces during fighting. Seemingly the opposing forces would be so frightened by the stone that they would simply lose courage and flee. Whether this ever really happened is not recorded.

Other small stones were also believed to bring good fortune rather than cure a specific condition. A blue stone, kept on the altar of the chapel of St Columba on Fladda, was said to bring good winds for sailors. The stone was always kept wet and sailors would wash the stone in a ceremonial manner to ensure they would get a suitable wind. The Kilchoman Cross on Islay has hollows at its base. In one of these hollows there is a stone which was to be turned in a sunwise direction while making a wish.

The Brahan Seer was said to have had a magical stone or pebble which gave him the power of prophecy.

*1. & 2. **Munlochy Well**, a clootie well on the Black Isle, which is still very popular today. Many items are left here, including rags, football shirts, shoes, and underwear. This place has a very strange and potent atmosphere.*

3. St Queran's Well, Islesteps. *The stone-lined well still has a flow of water, and is visited by many people.*

4. St Queran's Well, Islesteps. *The trees around the well are adorned with various items, including rings, ribbons, wind chimes and what appear to be written requests.*

5. Whitekirk. *This was once one of the most popular pilgrimage sites in Scotland. There was a well renowned for its miraculous cures near the church, but its location is now lost.*

6. St Fergus's Well, Glamis. *A signposted trail leads from the nearby Presbyterian church, demonstrating how attitudes have changed since the 17th and 18th centuries.*

*7. **St Anthony's Well, Holyrood Park.** The well (by the track to the right) was used for washing the face at sunrise on 1 May to improve looks. The ruins of St Anthony's Chapel lie to the left.*

*8. **St Triduana's Well (right of church).** The spring is located under the floor of the hexagonal building: requests for the well water, once popular for eye conditions, are still received.*

9. Cardinal's Hat Well, Stenton. *The holy well is located in a fine well house, shaped like a Cardinal's Hat, hence the name.*

10. St Margaret's Cave, Dunfermline. *The cave is located underneath a car park (reached down 87 steps), and was once Margaret's personal retreat.*

11. Kirkton of Aberfoyle with the Doon Hill in distance.
Reverend Robert Kirk is buried here – or is he trapped by fairies in the Doon Hill?

12. Eildon Hills. *Many legends are associated with these hills: the disappearance of True Thomas; the grave of Merlin the magician; and the haunt of the notorious wizard, Michael Scott.*

13. Minister's Tree, Doon Hill, Aberfoyle. *Reverend Robert Kirk died on the hill and may still be trapped here. Ribbons and rags are tied to branches: apparently a recent ritual.*

14. Lammer (Amber) Beads.

15. Elfshot.

16. Molluka Bean.

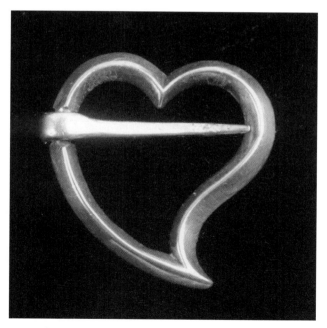

17. Silver Heart Brooch.

18. Dunvegan Castle, Skye. *Home to the famous Fairy Flag: a piece of Eastern silk, reputedly given to one of the MacLeod chiefs by his fairy wife.*

19. Fairy Bridge, Skye. *The meeting of roads and a burn, and where the MacLeod chief and his fairy wife are said to have parted forever: she had to return to her enchanted realm.*

20. Dunskey Castle.
Seat of the Adair family, and said to have once been the residence of a brownie.

21. Easdale Island. *The picturesque island, once the centre of slate production until a storm devastated the quarries, is also reputed to have been the abode of a brownie.*

22. Skipness Castle. *There are stories of a brownie or gruagach associated with Skipness, which describe her as a small golden-haired woman dressed in green.*

23. Falls of Dochart, Killin. *St Fillan is connected with Killin, and his healing stones are on display in the nearby Breadalbane Folklore Centre.*

24. Sheila na Gig, Rodel. *An unusual decoration for a church? The sexually-explicit carving is probably a pre-Reformation fertility symbol – another can be found at the nunnery on Iona.*

25. Baptism Well, Tarbat. *A conflation of Christian and magical belief: St Rule blessed the well, but a 'witch', Kirsty Bheag, used the water to baptise the son of the Earl of Cromartie.*

26. Demon, Stirling Castle. *The magical universe was populated by many spirits, both good and evil – elite belief had
witches in league with the Devil.*

27. North Berwick Auld Kirk. *This was reputedly the site of
the meeting of 'witches' at Hallowe'en in 1590 – starting the
infamous North Berwick witch trials.*

28. Esplanade (Castle Hill), Edinburgh Castle. *Now the site of the military tattoo, in previous centuries many people (perhaps 300) accused of witchcraft were throttled and burned here.*

29. Glamis Castle. *Janet Douglas, Lady Glamis, was accused of witchcraft and poisoning by James V and was burned alive on Castle Hill. Her ghost, a Grey Lady, is said to haunt Glamis.*

30. Maggie Walls Monument, Dunning. *Who was Maggie Walls? The writing is renewed and flowers are frequently left, yet there is no written evidence of such a person being executed. Perhaps her memorial is for all the victims of witchcraft trials.*

Witchcraft

WHAT IS WITCHCRAFT?

There are many Scottish stories and legends associated with witches and witchcraft. Some of them are based on real events and people – like the North Berwick witches in the 1590s, Isobel Gowdie from Auldearn in 1662, Agnes Finnie from Edinburgh executed in 1645 and Janet Corphat and others from Pittenweem in 1705. Other events or names may have been modified to make a better story or may even be apocryphal rather than actual. The story associated with Major Thomas Weir from Edinburgh who, it was claimed, was accused of bestiality, incest and witchcraft in 1670 is one such case. Weir was not, in fact, formally accused of witchcraft, although he was accused of the other two. His sister Jean did confess to, and was tried for, witchcraft and it is possible that the details from the two trials were later mistakenly combined. Gossip exaggerated the details and claimed that Thomas was accused of witchcraft – it probably also made a better story because he had been a member of an extremely strict religious sect called the Bowhead Saints, based around the West Bow in Edinburgh. Later ghost and haunting stories associated with that part of Edinburgh, and Weir, became part of local folklore.

The legend associated with the monument at Dunning in Perthshire is another example. It is claimed that the words on this stone commemorate the death of a local woman, Maggie Walls, who was executed for witchcraft in 1657 by being burnt alive – or so the story goes. Despite having being repeatedly cleaned the words re-appear. The problem is that there are no official documents naming anyone called Maggie Walls from Dunning or nearby. There may have been a woman called Maggie Walls who was executed illegally or it may be that the name is fictitious but was used to represent other women who were executed in the area.

The case of Kate MacNiven – the Witch of Monzie – is another confusing story about an alleged witch. Some local traditions claim that she was executed near Monzie in 1583 and there is a standing stone – known as Kate MacNieven's Stane – north of the Knock of Crieff. The dates and information about this person are, however, confusing: other dates given for her execution are 1615 and 1715. It is claimed that as Kate MacNiven was about to be burnt alive at the stake – which is itself unusual as in Scotland those found guilty were strangled before being burnt – the local laird, Graham of Inchbrackie, tried to stop events – to no avail. Before she died, however, in thanks Kate bit off one bead from her necklace and spat it at him, claiming that as long as his family kept it safe they would flourish. The bead remained a family heirloom for generations. Many of the details of the tale appear to come from Reverend George Blair, who was minister at Monzie in the 19th century, and most likely obtained this information from the descendants of the Grahams. Blair was eventually suspended from his post, and emigrated to Canada.

There was also another MacNiven or more accurately Nic Nevin – which means daughter of Nevin in Gaelic – who may have been a character from folk legend. Some accounts claimed that she was the queen of witches and may have been burned at St Andrews in 1569. Nic Nevin is mentioned later in the seventeenth century in the trials of other accused witches as a way to authenticate the accusations against them, notably John Brughe in 1643, but it is not clear if this was the same, or even a real, person.

There are both recorded and legendary stories about witches and witchcraft, but what was meant by witchcraft and who were witches? In the first section of the book the uses of beneficial witchcraft were discussed. This was used to counteract witchcraft that had caused harm or misfortune. It was used in healing, love magic, prophecy, finding lost or stolen goods and protection, and was sometimes referred to as white witchcraft. If beneficial, or white, witchcraft was needed to counteract negative effects, the implication was that something else had caused the harm. Generally this was thought to be harmful witchcraft, sometimes referred to as black witchcraft. This form of witchcraft and witch belief implied the use of some form of evil power, which was used for evil purposes to cause deliberate harm. This power was supernatural rather than natural. At the same time, however, witchcraft was used as an umbrella term: it referred to the general use of evil supernatural forces but it did not necessarily define how the forces were generated or used. Terms like sorcery and necromancy indicated more specifically the means by which evil power was manipulated.

The term witchcraft (in this case meaning harmful witchcraft) and others were used to denote certain beliefs and practices that were regarded as contrary to acceptable social norms or behaviour. Witches represented the opposite to everything that was considered as positive. Very few societies have not experienced, or recognised, the problem of witches and witchcraft at some point in their history. Attitudes and perceptions of witches and witchcraft have, however, changed over time, particularly in the industrialised West. This is the result of many cultural changes. In the West, witchcraft belief and practice is now regarded as primitive and currently we take it far less seriously than our ancestors did. In the past, however, our ancestors had very clear ideas about witchcraft and the natural world. Indeed witchcraft may have fulfilled a psychological need even though it played on people's fears. It permitted an explanation of misfortune that in turn could, potentially, be reversed. It incorporated both our past spiritual ideas and fantasies, and has continued to fulfil elements of current fantasies. Witches and witchcraft are currently a hot topic and related images pervade television, cinema, books and customs – albeit in as harmless a way as possible. Witchcraft appears to have a timeless ability to fit into whatever stereotype or idea that is currently popular.

Historical witchcraft in Western societies has very little to do with modern paganism, Wicca or new-age hedge witchcraft, all of which have developed partly as a result of a rejection of other religious belief systems. Although there are elements of pagan belief and ritual in their practice, much of it is based on a mistaken interpretation of the past or is a completely modern invention. Some of it is based on the false premise that witches in the past followed some form of female-dominated religious cult, often a fertility cult. Much of this inaccurate interpretation is the result of the work of Margaret Murray, an anthropologist, whose work *The Witch-Cult in Western Europe* was published in 1921, and which was then repeated in an article in *Encyclopedia Britannica*. She argued that witches were worshippers of an ancient cult of Diana and that their meetings were fertility rites. Murray chose her evidence selectively and subjectively, and omitted any details that did not correspond to, or contradicted, her ideas. She claimed that witches were organised in covens of thirteen, ignoring the evidence that showed that even if there were groups of this number there were just as many with smaller and larger numbers. Thirteen was, of course, a convenient number for Murray in that it demonstrated an inversion of Christian ritual and the Last Supper.

Murray interpreted the evidence very literally, denying the possibility that the confessions were the result of questioning and, in some cases, the use of torture. She did not acknowledge that both investigators and those being investigated shared cultural ideas. Some of those ideas were a conglomeration of popular cultural theories about magic and nature mixed with intellectual theories about the Devil and demonic witchcraft. Since popular ideas about magic have already been discussed, this section of the book will concentrate on intellectual theories about demonic witchcraft.

INTELLECTUAL DEMONOLOGICAL IDEAS

Since witchcraft was seen as a crime against society and God, it was prosecuted and persecuted by both religious and secular authorities. This meant that both theologians and judiciary interpreted, investigated and punished suspected use of demonic witchcraft. The harm that was perceived to have been caused by demonic witchcraft was important, but what was of prime importance was evidence of demonic involvement. This was what underpinned the intellectual arguments and theories about the threat of witchcraft and how it could be defeated. The intellectuals disseminated their theories and arguments through publications like *Malleus Maleficarum* by Sprenger and Kramer, *Daemonologie* by James VI and other similar works.

There are several arguments about why society attacked those they believed were witches. As far as religious authorities were concerned it was quite straightforward: technically anything that was regarded as being heterodox or heretical – opposed or opposite to the rules and regulations of the dominant religion of the time – could be categorised as witchcraft. It was, however, not quite as simple as this, as has been shown by the many elements of magical belief and practice that permeated social behaviour. The overriding feature of witchcraft that concerned the church was its relationship to the Devil. Equally the law was concerned with identifying and punishing it as a crime, so any evidence of harm – including bodily damage or loss of property – which was the result of demonic powers was important, although not crucial. Again the legal authorities were more concerned with the demonic element than actual harm.

Nevertheless, although the church and law provided the legal basis or framework on which many individuals were prosecuted for witchcraft, it was usually not the central authorities that instigated episodes of accusation and prosecution. There were some incidents where a local landowner or minister used an accusation of witchcraft to control or discipline a community. Even monarchs were not above personal involvement. James V accused Janet Douglas, Lady Glamis, of witchcraft and trying to poison the king in 1537. James VI was closely affected by the North Berwick trials in 1591-2. These circumstances were, however, relatively rare. Those who accused individuals of witchcraft were more likely to have been ordinary members of a community who would turn to the church and law in order to pursue their case. On many occasions it was perceived harm that led to the accusations. Some of those who were accused of witchcraft may have been a scapegoat figure: that is they were blamed for the misfortunes of others. Perhaps they had been a figure of suspicion or hate, often for many years and, if enough people felt aggrieved, it was possible to bring a case against them.

Although friends and neighbours may have been amongst the main accusers, the influence of the church and law should not, however, be understated. Local ministers, church elders and local lairds were very powerful and their attitude towards the crime of witchcraft was crucial. Many may have encouraged a climate of fear and distrust that would lead to accusations and pointing of fingers. On the other hand, others may have been discouraging and sceptical in their attitude, thus minimising any outbreaks of witch hunting in their area.

What made a witch a witch? The performance of harm or maleficium was one element but, as has been stated, the relationship with the Devil was extremely important. A witch was someone who had made a pact with the Devil and performed some form of tribute to him. The witch was regarded as inferior to the Devil, and was involved in diabolism or devil worship. It was believed that the witch derived her (the term her or she will be used as the majority of those who were accused in Scotland were female, but it should not be taken that all were) powers from the Devil as a result of the pact. Intellectuals produced pamphlets and books outlining their theories about Devil worship, the pact and the relationship between the Devil and witches.

The pact provided the legal basis of the crime and also explained the overlap between the harm that was caused by witchcraft and worship of the Devil. St Augustine discussed the idea that humans could make a pact with the Devil first, but his theory was not widely disseminated until the ninth century. At this time it was believed that the Devil and the human party (not necessarily a witch, at this time it was the relationship between magicians that was being examined) made a form of contract. This implied that, in return for the person's service and soul, the Devil would provide power or wealth. The pact was also linked with the early forms of learned magic. When Islamic and Greek books of magic were translated in the thirteenth century, the church authorities became increasingly concerned about their use. Although different types of magic, which have been described earlier, were practised, the authorities became increasingly convinced that all magicians were associated with the Devil. Magicians were seen as heretics and apostates.

This legal argument was initially applied to learned or high magic, but it could be, and was, extended to apply to all forms of magical practice. Simple protective or healing rituals could, and were, seen as being an aspect of the demonic pact. The Devil was the only power that was able to work magic therefore any human who claimed to have the ability to use magic of any sort must have made a pact with the Devil. As the concept of the demonic pact was extended to include those who practised popular or low magic, which included ordinary non-literate people, it was changed. The pact between magicians and the Devil was believed to be between two relatively equal parties. The pact between ordinary people and the Devil was quite different: the witch – rather than magician – was inferior and became the Devil's servant. At the same time, the gender of magical practitioner changed: the male magician became the female witch. Aristotle, and other Christian writers, claimed that women were the weaker sex. Women were both physically and morally weaker, and were more vulnerable to being tempted by the Devil. The prime, and first, example of a weak woman tempted by the Devil leading to the downfall of both herself and her man was, of course, Eve.

The pact that was negotiated between the Devil and a witch was a contract between master and servant. The witch was introduced to the Devil and agreed to serve him in return for rewards. The power to cause harm or have the Devil carry out harm was seen as important, but other rewards that were implied appear on the most part to have been relatively insignificant. Rather than huge wealth, new property or great beauty, in most cases the reward consisted of a few pennies – which often turned into stones – some food or drink or some new clothes. Janet Barker wanted to get the best red waistcoat from the Devil so that she could be the best-dressed servant in Edinburgh. Janet Morrison was offered property and wealth, which may have been more in keeping with the expected demonic rewards; but Alexander Hamilton was offered meat or clothing or money, but not all of them.

Demonologists believed that the witch made the pact during a meeting called a sabbat, where worship of the Devil took place. The *Malleus Maleficarum* stated that 'the witches meet together in conclave on a set day, and the devil appears to them in the assumed body of a man'. At these nocturnal meetings, witches indulged in various rituals, many of which were thought to be inversions of Christian worship. The theorists claimed that witches danced naked and carried out acts of infanticide and cannibalism. An important feature that was emphasised was the sexual element: it was claimed the Devil had intercourse with witches and the witches themselves indulged in promiscuous sex. There are accounts of sexual intercourse, although on most occasions it would appear to have been rather unpleasant. Isobel Murray said that she 'lay with a rough, black man', and Katherine Potter said that the Devil was as cold as ice. Margaret Lauder said the Devil lay with her in a beastly way like a dog

It was also believed that there was an inverted parody of holy communion: the witches renounced their baptism, accepted food and drink or recited prayers backward, although this latter element was not described in Scottish trials. Margaret Taylor renounced her baptism on her knees and Margaret Lauder agreed to quit Christ. Many others claimed that they had refused to renounce their baptism. Other indicators of the witches' rejection of Christianity were described in detail, such as being given a new name and receiving the Devil's mark. Many of the new names were quite mundane such as Thomas Shanks, who said his new name was Willie; Isobel Murray, who was to be called Lilbie; and Anna Kemp, whose new name was Janet. Others claimed to have had slightly more intriguing names such as Marion Grant who was called Dame, Catherine Skair whose new name was Isobel Fairweather and Agnes Williamson who was to be called Marie Luckifoot. It was claimed that the Devil's mark represented the teat on which the Devil, or the witch's familiar, would suck. Very often this mark was some insensitive skin tag or mole, and it would be located in a hidden part of the body: the underarm, neck or genital area. Most of the marks that were found were on the shoulder, neck or cheek but Margaret Duchill had one on her eyebrow, Isobel Young's was on her left breast and several, including Agnes Hendry, Janet Hendry, Isobel Inglis and Agnes Cairns, had marks found on or near their genitals or 'privy parts'.

Scottish witches also described giving themselves over 'body and soul' to the Devil, and there are a number of confessions were the accused reported that they had done this by symbolically touching their head and foot.

It was also believed that witches were able to fly and change shape. This explained how witches were able to attend sabbats when witnesses claimed they were at home or somewhere else. European accounts had witches travelling on pitchforks. This may have contributed to one of the most commonly held ideas in popular culture: the use of the broomstick by witches. There are a number of ways to interpret this motif: one is that the broomstick had phallic connotations, another that it was associated with fertility rites (jumping over a broomstick was believed to increase fertility), and thirdly that it symbolised the image of the female as brooms were more commonly associated with women than men. Flying on broomsticks was rare in Scotland – Isabel Gowdie from Auldearn mentioned flying on a piece of straw – but there were examples from other countries. James VI explained how the Devil as a spirit was able to move witches who were solid material, but acknowledged that it could only be for short journeys as they would not be able to hold their breath for long periods. He also wrote that while witches were being transported they were invisible to everyone but themselves.

Changing shape or metamorphosis was another belief that was associated with witchcraft, although it was described relatively infrequently by the confessing witches. The most typical included Bessie Thom who described hares and cats, Margaret Duchill who mentioned dogs and cats and Isobel Robie whose confession included details about hares. More unusual were Marion Veitch and Isobel Eliot who both described bumble bees. Marion Veitch also mentioned corbies or crows and Marion Peebles was the only one who mentioned a pellock whale or porpoise – a probably unique form. There are local folk tales that describe witches appearing in other forms, including wolves, hares and birds, but few confessions include references to this kind of detail. Again James VI had an explanation for this ability. He claimed that while witches were in another form – often that of a beast or bird – they were able to pass through doors or windows even if they were shut.

DEVILS AND DEMONS

The descriptions of the Devil and other demons varied quite a lot. Sometimes they fitted the stereotypical image of a horned and cloven-hoofed dark beast but on other occasions the Devil appeared in the shape of an animal or even just an ordinary man. Nevertheless, the figure of the Devil that featured in much of the documentary material associated with witchcraft is a more complex being than might have been anticipated. The Devil has a number of epithets – Auld Nick, Satan, Lord of the Flies, Lucifer, the Earl of Hell, Mahoun – and could take a number of forms.

Demonic figures were often male who were clad in black, but they could also wear other colours including blue, brown, grey and white. The colour green was mentioned quite often, and could also be associated with fairies or 'good neighbours' although, as discussed earlier, they were not always good! The figures could be old or young, handsome or ugly, or they could be grim or pleasant. The demon could wear a hat or bonnet, a shawl or hood, or carry a staff. He could offer food, drink or some other relatively small-scale reward. The demonic figure could also appear in female form, albeit quite rarely, or take the form of an animal. Sometimes the animal forms later changed into human form.

Finally, he could take a more ethereal guise and appear as a spirit – sometimes as a ghost or angel. In this form the demonic figure could also appear as a meteorological manifestation. Some cases refer to whirlwinds, which would then take the shape of a man.

The existence of the Biblical and Christian version of the Devil was well documented and acknowledged by theologians and others, but even these writers recognised that the whole area of demonic belief was complex. James VI wrote that the Devil could appear in different forms: those who troubled houses and solitary places, those who troubled or followed people, those who possessed people, and those who were called fairies.

One form of demon was referred to as *spectra* or *lemures* – spirits of the dead or ghosts. These could inhabit a dead body and use it to communicate and move about. The Devil also could deceive ignorant people into believing he could appear as an angel, particularly the angel of light or Lucifer. Other forms of spirits known as incubi and succubi – spirits that inhabited the 'northern and barbarous parts of the world' rather than the 'southern, civilised world' – either appeared as a spirit or borrowed the body of a dead person in order to have sex with humans. The Devil could possess people and those who were possessed had certain physical and emotional symptoms. They would be repulsed by religious symbols such as Holy water or the sign of the cross; they would scream at readings from the Bible; their stomachs would swell; they might vomit stones or other objects; and they would sometimes speak in strange languages. According to James, this happened in places like Lapland, Finland, Orkney and Shetland where ignorance and barbarity was at its greatest – which seems a little harsh. Fairies or 'good neighbours' were believed to be another form of demon. James wrote that they were associated with Diana, there was a king and queen and an attendant court and they rode, drank and moved like ordinary men and women. One form of demon that did not seem to exist in Scotland, however, was that of a werewolf. Lycanthropy was not a real manifestation, according to James, but merely a result of too much melancholy causing men to imagine that they had changed into wolves. When they were in a fit they would move on their hands and knees and attempt to attack people as an animal would do. This type of behaviour was not supernatural or spiritual, but was entirely physical and a result of an imbalance of humours, which could be treated medically. However, in middle and Eastern European communities, particularly those located in heavily forested areas, there were people who claimed to be able to transform themselves into wolves or other beasts.

A man in black was the most common form of Devil mentioned, and typical descriptions of men in black are illustrated by Alexander Hamilton, executed for witchcraft in 1630, who described a black man in black clothes who did not have a cloak but had a wand. Agnes Clarkson, accused of witchcraft in 1649, described meeting a black man with a staff. Janet Morrison confessed in 1662 to seeing the Devil as a naked man with a black head and another black man who was rough and fierce. Margaret Jackson, executed for witchcraft in 1677, described a black man with a bluish band and white cuffs, who wore hoggers (a stocking worn as a gaiter), but no shoes.

The colour green was frequently associated with fairies. Some descriptions simply refer to 'a man in green', and make no direct reference to (or use the terms) elf or fairy. Equally green was not the only colour that was mentioned in connection with fairies. Isobel Smith, tried for witchcraft in 1661, described a black man dressed in green, combining both demonic and fairy elements. In 1616, Elspeth Riach claimed that she met a male devil in green tartan. She also said that she met another male, this time a male fairy that she claimed was her relative. The male fairy in Isobel Haldane's account from 1623 had a grey beard. Barbara Parish, from Livingston, who was probably executed in 1647, confessed that she met a male fairy in green clothing with a grey hat. In 1662, Isobel Gowdie described meeting a well-favoured man who was the King of Fairies at the church of Auldearn.

As discussed earlier, the 'good neighbours' or fairies were difficult to categorise. James VI and theologians equated fairies with demons. For others, the relationship may not have been so obvious. Although the Devil was evil and harmful, fairies were not so easy to define. Some fairies or elves could, and did, cause harm, but generally they were seen as neutral or morally ambiguous. They could use their powers for both good and bad, depending on circumstances. Andrew Man and Isobel Haldane both got their skill in healing from the fairies, but Alison Pearson was punished by them and lost the power of one side of her body. Those who confessed to meeting fairies rather than the Devil would appear either to have distinguished between different types of demons or were using different words or ideas to describe the same thing.

Demons could also appear as ghosts. Janet Boyman, executed in 1572, claimed that the Devil appeared to her in the spirit of Maggie Dewand, a woman who was known to her. In 1576 Bessie Dunlop claimed she met a number of ghosts: the ghosts of Thomas Reid, said to have died at the battle of Pinkie in 1547, and the Laird of Auchenskeith. In 1598 Andrew Man confessed to meeting a wide range of spirits in various forms including the ghosts of Thomas the Rhymer and James IV, as well as a black beast. In 1605 Patrick Lawrie from Dundonald claimed he met the spirit of the deceased Helena McBurnie. Margaret Jackson claimed she met the spirit, or ghost, of her dead husband, Thomas Stewart.

Devils and demons were a crucial element in witchcraft belief and prosecution. The presence of the Devil was important to prosecutors because it confirmed the guilt of the accused witch. Details of confessions, describing the Devil in different shapes, guises and forms, combined popular ideas about spirits with theories that had been outlined by intellectual demonologists. This created a stereotypical image of demonic witchcraft that perpetuated throughout the period of witch hunting and beyond.

Harm, Bad Luck and Spells

Although demonic features were important to the prosecuting authorities, the harm, which was thought to be caused by witches, was also very important to the process of accusation. It was claimed that witches received the power to cause harm as a reward for becoming the Devil's servant. The type of harm or malefice that could be caused included the spoiling of milk or ale, the failure of a crop to ripen, any illness or injury in an animal or person and the death of an animal or human. Witches were believed to influence people's choice of lover, to cause impotence and to cause hailstorms, tempests and lightning.

Those who were accused of, or confessed to, using witchcraft to cause harm reportedly used a variety of spells, charms, rituals, potions and curses. These seem to have involved a combination of visual, oral and operative features. They stuck pins in wax figures and occasionally administered potions made from herbs, plants and animal parts. Stones, pieces of meat and knots were also used to cause harm or injury. Objects or items were stolen from the intended victim and used to inflict harm. They spoke words and carried out acts in a precise order or manner. Janet Stratton and others from North Berwick used the melted remains of a toad to wreck the king's ship. They also walked three times in a withershins or anti-sunwise direction to make the spell work. Christine Lewinstoun or Livingston, executed for witchcraft in 1597, said she used herbs, hair, thread and nail trimmings and that she had received her skill and knowledge from the fairies.

One assumption was that witches would use magic circles as a visual element in their performance of magic. These would be geometrical forms – circles and triangles – with some words or characters around the circumference. Sometimes these would be scriptural extracts or representations of God. They could be quite simple or extremely complex and were used to conjure spirits or demons. This type of magic was categorised as necromancy, and there were many books and manuscripts, produced between the thirteenth and fifteenth centuries, which illustrated a range of different magic circles that could be used to summon demons in different forms. This type of magic was, however, very specialised and was used by literate magicians rather than non-literate witches. Most witches did not have access to these forms of manuals and, although some of those who were accused of witchcraft were also accused of necromancy, there is no indication in the confessions or accusations of the use of magic circles. Possibly some of the accused witches may have used some form of circle in order to cause chaos or harm – perhaps walking in a withershins direction – but there is relatively little specific evidence of this being done in Scotland between the sixteenth and eighteenth centuries.

It may also have been thought that some witches made brews containing 'eye of newt and toe of frog, wool of bat and tongue of dog' but it would seem that they probably did less of this than Shakespeare implied. There were, however, plenty other methods using visual and operative elements which they could use to cause harm. They could steal the milk of cows by sitting down in their own homes and 'milking' a knife or stick. They would use the knife or stick to symbolise the cow, and the milk would be transferred from a nearby cow to the witch. Sometimes a tether that had been used with the animal or one of its tail hairs would be used for the same effect. Isobel Gowdie said that she could steal milk by passing a tether between the animal's legs. Catherine MacTaggert, found guilty in 1688, said she threw a hair tether into a neighbour's house who later became ill. Patrick Lawrie, executed in 1605, had a hair belt that he used to harm or damage cow's milk and Isobel Houston, who was tried in 1700, was accused of milking a leather strap like a cow to steal other people's milk.

To cause rain or hailstorms the witch would dip a piece of wood in water and sprinkle the water in the air. Wax figures were made of intended victims in order to bewitch them or cause them harm. These were sometimes baked or placed in a fire to cause the victim to suffer bouts of extreme fever. Similarly, those who intended harm could use hair or nail clippings, which were also often used in healing rituals. In order to prevent them being used by witches, disposal of hair and nail trimming was important: the most commonly used method was burial. Those who wished to cause harm could also leave pieces of raw meat at the door or threshold of their enemy. This was often the door to the animal byre, as it was believed that as the meat rotted the curse would transfer to the animals and they would become ill. Janet Leisk, tried in 1597, plucked three feathers from a goose then blew on them and the goose later died. Katherine Oswald, executed in 1629, urinated on nettles; and Alison Dick, executed in 1633, urinated outside a neighbour's meal cellar and ruined the meal. Margaret Hutchison, eventually executed in 1661, put raw flesh under the door of her intended victim.

These methods use both sympathy and contiguity. The object used either represented the victim or outcome – often in appearance – or it had had some physical connection or contact. The knife or stick represented the cow's udder, and the tether would have been used with the cow and so would have had physical contact. Water sprinkled in the air symbolised the rain or storm. The wax figures represented a person, and hair and nail clippings had belonged to an individual and so had a strong physical link to them. Sometimes the two were combined and the hair or nail clippings would be incorporated into the wax figure so that it was clear who the victim was.

Other objects that were more reminiscent of Shakespeare's ideas were used at times. Isobel Gowdie said that she used the corpse of an unbaptised baby in a ritual. She claimed that she used nail clippings, meal and kale, which were all chopped finely and mixed with the corpse. The resulting concoction was then buried under dung heaps in a neighbour's land. The neighbour then lost his crop, and Isobel and her companions gained the profit – they benefited from the meal – which they were able to use to feed their families. Other accused witches confessed to using bits of animals or corpses in their spells. Agnes Sampson confessed to collecting the venom of a toad in order that she, and the others involved in the North Berwick trial, could harm James VI.

The other important factor was the combination of physical, visual elements and ritual observance. How the objects were used was sometimes more important than the object itself. Words were, however, also important and, like healing charms, they often took the form of standard Christian prayers or at least borrowed heavily from them. Their use would, however, be irreverent. The prayer or conjuration may have been recited a set number of times in a particular direction or manner. The words were uttered imperatively as a command, rather than as an appeal or request. Again, like magic circles the evidence for this use is limited and really applied to magicians rather than some poor illiterate witch. It can be seen, however, that the authorities might, and did, interpret the use of healing prayers as conjuring and so categorised them as a form of necromancy.

There was another more frequent use of words: they were often uttered as a verbal curse or malison. The power of the tongue was often mightier than the sword, and many women were experts in verbal insults. The words that were used were often not recorded in the evidence but other documents and examples can give a flavour of the type of insult that was bandied about. Agnes Finnie was accused of cursing Janet Grinton, who later took a serious illness and died, having not eaten for a fortnight. Agnes and Janet had argued over the quality of fish that Agnes had sold – Janet claimed it was not fresh. In retaliation Agnes shouted at Janet 'God your way home, you shall not eat more again in this world'. Agnes had also cursed John Buchanan 'John, go away, for as you have begun with witches, so shall you end with witches'. He was ill for seven weeks after this dispute. Agnes also argued with Euphamie Kincaid, who Agnes called a drunk. Euphamie retaliated by claiming 'If I am a drunkard, you are a witch'. Agnes's response was 'If I am a witch either you or yours shall have better cause to call me so'. Two days later Euphamie's daughter had broken her leg. Agnes also shouted at another woman, Margaret Williamson, 'The devil ride blow you blind' and later Williamson lost the sight of her left eye. It seemed to the community and those involved in the trial that Agnes's words were both curses and prophecies, as she was found guilty.

Many incidents of cursing and arguing were recorded in town and church records. Those involved often complained to the authorities to get them to intervene in order to settle a dispute or both parties could be reported for brawling or flyting as it was termed. Tit-for-tat insults were exchanged: 'you bitch', 'you thief', 'you whore', 'you witch', 'you witch's gyte' (child of a witch) – and sometimes all of these together. On most occasions, however, these incidents were not treated as an accusation or identification of a witch. Nor indeed were these insults regarded as harmful curses or malisons. They were a private dispute that had been played out in public and quite often both parties were reprimanded.

Undoubtedly murder was the most serious outcome of a witch's actions. In some cases, the death of a victim would appear to have been the intended outcome of those who were accused of witchcraft. In other cases, however, the death of a person may have been the end result but it may have happened by accident – perhaps through the transference of an illness from one person to another. There were some occasions where a murder was attempted – and sometimes succeeded – in order to gain property or titles. On other occasions, there may have been an element of revenge involved. Katherine Ross, Lady Fowlis, and her younger stepson attempted a complicated double murder in the 1590s. Lady Fowlis and Hector planned to murder Hector's brother Robert so that Hector could inherit the title of baron of Fowlis. Lady Fowlis also planned to murder her sister-in-law, Marjory Campbell, in order that her brother – George Ross – could then marry Robert's wealthy widow. In this case neither Lady Katherine nor Hector were accused of being witches themselves, but of having consulted others for spells and magic in order to cause the deaths. Lady Fowlis threw elfshot or arrows at images of her sister-in-law and stepson which were made of butter.

Although Lady Fowlis used witchcraft as a means to achieve her objective, she also used more pragmatic methods, particularly poisoning. Unfortunately people other than the intended victims also suffered when the poisoned food was eaten accidentally. Lady Fowlis, although tried for witchcraft and poisoning, escaped punishment as the case against her was first found not proven and at a second trial she was found not guilty.

The Erskine of Dun family was involved in a particularly nasty case of murder and attempted murder in the seventeenth century. The grandchildren of Robert Erskine of Dun, one of the leaders of the Reformation in 1560, were accused of the crime in 1613-14. Robert Erskine and his three sisters – Helen, Isobel and Annas – attempted to murder their nephews, John and Alexander, in 1610. Robert had been deprived of the financial benefits of tutoring his nephews, who were in line to inherit the title and lands. Two of the sisters went to a local woman – Janet Irving – who had a reputation for being a witch. She gave them herbs to soak in ale, which would poison the boys. They were given the poisoned ale and soon began to vomit. The older boy, John, developed a terrible disease – his skin turned black (possibly some form of gangrene), 'his inward parts were consumed' and he remained in great distress until he died. The younger boy, Alexander, was also severely ill but he survived and inherited the title. Robert, Isobel and Annas were tried and executed, while Helen was banished and fled to Orkney.

It would seem in these cases that although witchcraft was used as a means to procure the intended outcome, the perpetrators – or those who advised them – were also quite practical and, as well as using magical actions and objects, they also used poison to harm their victims. Perhaps they did not think the witchcraft would be powerful enough and that poison would be more reliable.

On occasion an accusation of witchcraft could be used politically. As seen by the charges of witchcraft and poisoning that were made against Janet Douglas, Lady Glamis by James V. As a child James V had been brought up for some years – some suggest against his will – in the household of his step-father Archibald Douglas, sixth Earl of Angus. When he finally asserted himself, James took his revenge on the Douglas family, and Janet appears to have been an innocent victim. She was burned alive on the Castle Hill in Edinburgh. James VI later accused Francis Stewart, the fifth Earl of Bothwell, of witchcraft after he had fallen out of favour with the king.

Revenge was a reason for murder or attempted murder, but the perpetrators did not always gain financial or other rewards, as in the Fowlis and Erskine examples. The accused may have caused the harm because there had been an exchange of insults, non-payment of debts, or some other perceived dissatisfaction against the victim. Sir George Maxwell of Pollok was said to have been the victim of an attempted murder by a group of people in 1676. Janet Mathie, her son and daughter John and Annabelle Stewart, Margaret Jackson, Bessie Weir and Marjory Craig all confessed to demonic pact and carrying out rituals with wax images in order to cause harm to Sir George who was their landlord. Isobel Grierson, executed in 1607, had an 'evil will' against William Burnet and used devilish and ungodly means to rid him of his life. She threw a piece of raw enchanted meat at his door and afterwards the Devil appeared in the shape of a naked child every night for six months. When William named the apparition using Isobel's name, it vanished but he took a serious illness that lasted three years until he died in 'great dolour and payne'.

Some of those who were accused of causing death by witchcraft were requested to do so by others. In these cases the revenge was not personal from the point of view of the accused witch. Someone else used the skills and knowledge of the witch to settle a dispute. In 1603, Janet Christie and her mother were accused of having requested James Reid to bewitch David Liberton, his wife and their goods and property. To do this Reid made nine cuts in a piece of raw meat and told Christie to put some under the door of Liberton's mill and the rest under the stable door in order to destroy his business and animals. He also enchanted nine stones, which he threw over Liberton's land in order to destroy Liberton's crops. Reid made a wax image of Liberton that Christie and her mother turned in a fire in an attempt to destroy Liberton. Reid was eventually executed.

In the unsettled and difficult years of the seventeenth century, economic pressures affected both those suspected of witchcraft and those around them. Failure to settle debts or some form of perceived insult were certainly reasons for vindictiveness, but the ultimate objective may not have been to cause permanent harm or death but rather to make a point – possibly extract an apology or repayment of debt. In these cases the harm could be reversed, either by the malicious witch who was thought to have caused the harm or by a beneficial witch who might have had a reputation as a charmer. Sometimes the 'curse' or harm was removed after the victim had apologised or the dispute had been settled. Robert Pedan took a severe illness and remained sick for over a year. He then remembered that he owed Isobel Grierson nine shillings and four pennies but had refused to pay it. Grierson had then uttered curses and told Pedan he would regret it. Pedan finally repaid the money and three times asked her to restore his health: within twenty-four hours, he had recovered. Helen Keir, from Clackmannan, had asked for some food from Alexander Mitchie, which was refused. She cursed his daughter who immediately fell sick. Mitchie's wife then went to Keir and threatened her with a knife, whereupon Keir's daughter cured the child. Robert Horner called Keir a witch and immediately his child fell ill and died, and later he contracted a sickness, which was cured by another woman, Janet Tailor, who identified Keir as the cause of his troubles.

As well as deliberate murder or malefice, accidental death or harm as a result of actions by suspected witches featured among accusations. This occurred if the suspected witch had been involved in removing an illness from one person but which had then been transferred to another person or animal. Quite often they were not malicious witches. Thomas Grieve, executed in 1623, took a sickness off a woman, which was then transferred onto her cow and which proceeded to run mad and die. Steven Maltman, or Malcolm, was asked to cure Janet Christie of a sickness. He instructed her husband to collect some south running water and put a stone in it. The water was then given to the woman but Maltman was accused of having transferred the disease to her servant Agnes Davidson. These witches really seem to have been charmers – beneficial witches – whose practices unfortunately got them into trouble. This was perhaps because their communities were afraid of them, felt troubled by their power, or because their recommendations had negative consequences.

HUNTING THE WITCH

The parliament of 1563 passed the first official Witchcraft Act in Scotland, although witchcraft had been used as an accusation against individuals before that date. According to some accounts, the last person to be executed for witchcraft under the wording of this Act was in 1727. This case is poorly documented and the date is not even certain. According to Edmund Burt, who worked in the Highlands in the early eighteenth century, two women from the parish of Loth in Sutherland were tried and condemned for witchcraft and the mother, Janet Horne, was burnt at Dornoch. It was claimed that she was able to transform her daughter into a pony in order that she could ride on her to meetings with other witches. It was said that the Devil shod the girl while she was in the form of a pony and this had caused her to be lame. According to the inscription on the Witch's Stone in Dornoch, the date was 1722.

Although the Witchcraft Act was modified in 1736 it was not removed from the statute, nor did the belief in witchcraft disappear. The reworded act stated that individuals could be prosecuted for pretending to be a witch or carry out witchcraft. Indeed during the eighteenth century, kirk sessions and others noted some incidents of people carrying out healing or protective rituals, although they were not accused of witchcraft per se. In some of these later cases the individuals were accused of 'pretending to exercise witchcraft, sorcery, inchantment, conjuration etc'.

Indeed, the last person to be charged under the act was during the Second World War. Helen Duncan, originally from Callander, claimed to be a spiritualist and medium. During a séance she said that she had communicated with a sailor who had been killed at sea. At the time the Home Office had not issued any information about the sinking of the sailor's ship for fear of damaging morale. The Government of the day accused Duncan of spying and she was found guilty and imprisoned.

Throughout the years between 1563 and 1736 there were around 4000 people accused of witchcraft in Scotland. Exact totals are hard to calculate as the documentary evidence is often incomplete or vague. The number of people who were executed is also quite difficult to calculate as the verdicts and sentences were not always recorded, and there may even have been the occasional trial and execution that did not have official permission.

The official legal action through which those who were accused of witchcraft were processed could be quite a long and complicated business. On other occasions, however, the process could be relatively rapid. Not all investigations and witchcraft trials followed the same route, but there were features that were common to many.

Although the church and state provided the official framework for prosecution, the first stage involved accusations from other people – often neighbours and friends from the local community or nearby communities. These were most often people who were known to the accused person. Sometimes accusers were other accused witches who named them as their accomplices during their confessions. The first official body that was involved was either the church or the local laird. The kirk session – comprising the minister and elders – would call witnesses and interview the accused. Local council officials might also be involved, although many of them were also members of the kirk session.

At this point counter accusations might be made by the accused – perhaps in an attempt to claim a case of slander. The statements of the witnesses and the accused were assessed. If the evidence was not too complicated the kirk session could reprimand the individual, for example if it was an episode of slander. If the evidence was a bit more complicated, the kirk session could refer to the presbytery for advice. The presbytery would review the evidence and decide on the next stage. If the case did not involve the Devil – the accused was perhaps only using simple magical rituals for protection or healing – the case could remain within the jurisdiction of the church. The punishment that was issued by the church usually took the form of public penance: the guilty person would appear in sackcloth before the local congregation and might also pay a fine.

If the accused did not comply or the church officials were unhappy that the accused had not satisfied their conditions – for example continuing to use magic – they could excommunicate those involved. Even those who may have tried to move away from a parish could not always escape the discipline of the church. The church was a powerful mechanism of social control in the seventeenth century, and the amount of exchange of information that went on between different kirk sessions and ministers was remarkable. Individuals who appeared in a new community needed to produce testaments of good character and behaviour. If these documents were not produced, they could be ordered back to their original parish. Kirk sessions could also be asked to search, or keep a look out, for people who had absconded from another parish. This meant that theoretically those who failed to observe the authority of the church might find it difficult to find safe hiding elsewhere but, nevertheless, there is evidence that people did manage to escape censure and disappear.

If the evidence was more ominous and demonic involvement was suspected, the accused would be questioned – often repeatedly – and may have been held in ward or imprisoned during this time. The accused could appear at their own recognisance or they could be held in the nearest tolbooth, in the church itself – sometimes the steeple – or in a house, either their own or some other person's. Technically permission from the state was required before an individual could be held, but in many cases this was applied retrospectively. The purpose of the repeated questioning was to elicit a confession. Accusations of harm, or a bad reputation, were not in themselves sufficient proof. The authorities needed a confession of the demonic pact as it was regarded as the key piece of evidence. Details about rituals that were used to cause harm and destruction or elements of folk culture, such as fairy beliefs or festivals, were useful but not of primary importance to the legal and church authorities. To extract the confession some form of torture would often be used. The most common method of psychological torture was sleep deprivation, although there is evidence that other forms of direct torture were used, including thumbscrews, removal of nails, and the application of the boots to crush ankles and feet.

Another frequently used method of torture or ordeal, which was used to extract an admission but also to identify guilt, was the process of pricking. Prickers were individuals who were known by their reputation to be able to identify a witch by locating the Devil's marks on her body. Prickers would travel the country and were employed by local communities to examine suspects and search for the Devil's mark by inserting needles into suspicious marks or moles. This was in order to find out whether or not the accused could feel pain at these places. It was claimed that if these spots did not bleed, or no pain was felt, then this proved the suspect was guilty. According to the prickers, the marks were said to be located under the arms, on the neck or in the genital area, and this involved extensive and humiliating examination. Many of the accused confessed to having marks without having been pricked, but just as many were pricked in front of male witnesses – usually members of the kirk session. It is thought that some of the prickers may have been women but the names of those recorded are all male.

Latterly even the authorities began to question the prickers' dubious practice, and it was suspected that they were mountebanks or charlatans. Some of them used a needle that retracted when pressed into the skin. Some of them 'encouraged' their victims to name a lot of other people in return for promises of lesser punishment, in order to extend their employment: prickers were often paid by the number of guilty people they identified. George Cathie appears to have encouraged Janet Coutts from Peebles, who was executed in 1650, to name upwards of 88 people. Some of them were from Biggar and Coutts was taken from Peebles to Biggar to confront them in the church where, luckily for them, she confessed that she had lied. By the mid-seventeenth century a number of prickers were imprisoned and ordered to stop.

At any stage, those involved at local level could, and should, have made a request to the central authorities to get a commission of justiciary. Commissions could be issued by the king, Parliament or the Privy Council or, for a short time after 1649, the Committee of Estates, and could take the form of commission of investigation, investigation and trial, or just a trial, as well as for the use of torture. Before any torture was used, those involved should have requested a commission but this was often ignored. Other options that were available to the central authorities – and one that was used on occasion – was either a dismissal, on the grounds that there was not adequate evidence, in which case the charges were to be dropped and the suspect released, or that the pursuers were to get more evidence.

A commission named a group of six or so men, who were given permission to gather more evidence. In many cases they may well have already been involved in the investigation. The commission would include local lairds or landowners, ministers, town provosts, bailies and clerks, lawyers and schoolteachers. The local sheriff was also often a member of a commission and a centrally appointed lawyer was often named.

The trial could be held at the Central Court of Justiciary in Edinburgh, at one of the Circuit Courts, which covered the rest of the country, or at a locally organised court. In the second half of the seventeenth century, the central authorities would send out centrally-appointed Justice Deputes to oversee the courts, rather than rely on the elite members of local communities. Most trials were held locally, as this was the cheapest option. Some local stories, perhaps folkloric, mention stones or commemorative areas where witches were reputedly executed, as seen at Spott and Abernethy, as well as Dornoch, Dunning and Crieff.

At the trial, witnesses were called and juries appointed and the process followed the legislation of the time. There were, however, some areas of protocol that were exceptional for the time or very different from current practice. Women were permitted to be witnesses; the usual practice was that they were not allowed to be. Although this was exceptional, it was claimed that the kind of incident, particularly illness and death, associated with witchcraft would have involved the experience of women and so the rules were altered. Those who may have had a personal grudge, who claimed that the suspect had harmed them, were allowed to appear as prosecution witnesses. Circumstantial evidence or hearsay was admissible – points were made based on reputation and local information rather than eye-witness accounts. Members of the jury were very likely to have had personal association with both sides since they were appointed from local communities.

Some of those who had trials did have defence lawyers, who tried to object to witnesses or jury members. They argued that there was often not sufficient proof of guilt or that many of the incidents could be explained by natural misfortune and events rather than caused by any supernatural intervention. Some lawyers began to question the reality of magic and magical powers. Most juries, however, convicted on the basis of the confession, which the accused had usually made before they got to trial. Nevertheless, some of the accused continued to proclaim their innocence and denied the accusations. They also claimed that their confessions were false. Lawyers tried to apply for acquittal or abandonment of a trial on the grounds of age, infirmity, pregnancy or mental incompetence. Sometimes the trial did not take place because the accused died in prison, either from natural causes or by their own hand, or they managed to escape and evaded recapture.

If the accused was found guilty then the most common sentence was death. The guilty were to be strangled then burnt; only a few were burned alive. Not all of those who were tried were found guilty: some were found not guilty or were found guilty on only some of the charges. If they were not guilty of the most serious accusations then a court could order them to be banished – although difficult, banishment was undoubtedly a preferable option to execution.

The financial cost of investigation, trial and execution was borne by the local community; the state did not provide financial support. Any property that the accused owned – and very often this was very little – was not shared out among the locals but was secured by the state. The cost of holding the accused; paying for wardens to keep watch; the cost of having letters of application written and delivered, which involved the cost of a man and horse to ride to Edinburgh; payment for lawyers and other court officials; the fee charged by the prickers; and, finally, the hangman's pay and the price of the fuel used in the fire all contributed to an expensive process. Costs for Alison Dick's trial and execution in 1633 included money for getting the commission, supplying waistcoats for the men who were trying the accused, coal, barrels and ropes for the execution, and payment for the executioner.

It is a commonly held misapprehension that it was easy to accuse, try and execute suspects for witchcraft. In fact the opposite was true. Accusations were not made lightly. It was a serious crime, and prosecutions were only undertaken when there was convincing evidence to pursue the matter. Modern audiences may criticise the whole belief system and, at the same time, condemn those who were involved in the prosecution of suspects, while forgiving those who claimed to have practised witchcraft. Those who participated in witch trials were as much part of the same society as those they investigated: they all held the same beliefs in magic and the supernatural. The legal system might be criticised because it did not comply with modern accepted contemporary practice, but most cases appear to have followed the legislation of the time. There were some extremely distressing exceptions, and these cannot be excused, but the fear of witchcraft permeated all levels of society – not just the church – and, as with all social concerns, society was anxious to rid itself of the cause. Witchcraft was a metaphor for the overall anxiety that affected seventeenth century society. Witchcraft was not the cause of civil and religious upheaval, neither was it caused by the disruption that occurred as a result, but it was something that could be targeted because it was such a fundamental, if vulnerable, aspect of behaviour and belief.

Places of Interest

Map: Places of Interest

A	B	C	D	E	F	G	H

1

Noltland• North Ronaldsay•

ORKNEY

2

Brodgar• Kirkwall•
Stenness• •Tankerness

3

Crosskirk•
•Thurso
•Wick
Mid Clyth•

Eoropie•

Callanish•
•Stornoway

LEWIS

4

HARRIS

Dornoch•

•St Kilda •Rodel •Loch Maree Fodderty• •Tarbat
Laiaval• NORTH UIST •Loch Siant Burghead•Hopeman
5 •Carinish •Trumpan Munlochy• •Navity •Portnockie
•Fairy Bridge Portree• Craigiehowe• •Elgin
Dunvegan• •Applecross Inverness•Culloden •Auldearn Orton Chapel of Seggat•
Dumeath• Huntly•

SOUTH SKYE Williamston• •Knockandy Hill
UIST •Auchindour

6

•Ben Newe Aberdeen•
Kincardine O'Neil• Stonehaven•

House of Dun•

•Fort William •Tigh an Tobar •Montrose
7 Glamis• •Forfar
Inchadney•
Dunstaffnage• •Dalvuie •Tillichuil
•Strontoiller Wester Lix •Killin Dundee• •Claypotts
Oban• •Monzie Perth•
MULL Luing• Balquhidder• Dunfillan• •St Andrews
8 Kintraw• Dunning• Abernethy•
Colonsay House• •Inverliever Aberfoyle• •Glendevon
COLONSAY Ballymeanoch• Kirkton Stirling• Dunfermline• North Berwick•
JURA Pitreavie• Aberdour• •Whitekirk
Kilchoman• Gourock• Linlithgow• Haddington• •Spott
•Glasgow Edinburgh• Stenton•
9 •ISLAY Skipness• Kilallan• Carnwath• •Innerleithen
•Kingarth Lanark• Peebles• •Kelso
ARRAN Darvel• Lamington Minch Moor •Eildon Hills
Carterhaugh•
•Ayr Hawick•

10

•Penpont

•Dalry Dumfries•

Islesteps•
Stranraer• •Kilhern Moss •Barskeoch Hill
11 •Dunskey •Crouse

•Mull of Galloway

108

LIST OF PLACES OF INTEREST

Abernethy F8
Applecross C5
Auldearn Church F5
Ballymeanoch Standing Stones C8
Balquhidder Kirk E8
Ben Newe F6
Braemou Well, Hopeman F5
Breadalbane Folklore Centre,
  Killin E7
Burghead F5
Callanish Standing Stones (HS)
  B3
Carnwath Church F9
Chapel Well, Chapel of Seggat G5
Chapel Wells, Mull of Galloway
  Farm D11
Cheese Well, Minch Moor F9
Claypotts Castle (HS) F7
Colonsay House Gardens C8
Craigiehowe Cave E5
Dagon Stone, Darvel E9
Doon Hill, Aberfoyle E8
Dow Loch, Penpont E10
Dunskey Castle D11
Dunstaffnage Castle (HS) C7
Dunvegan Castle B5
Edinburgh Castle (HS) F9
Eildon Hills G9
Fairy Bridge B5
Forfar G7
Glamis Castle F7
Glamis Well, Church and Pictish
  Stone F7
Glendevon Parish Church F8
Hill o' Many Stanes, Mid Clyth
  (HS) F3
Hole Stone, Crouse E11
Hole Stone, Dalry E10
Holyrood Park, Edinburgh (HS)
  F9

House of Dun, Montrose (NTS)
  G7
Inchadney E7
Isle Maree, Loch Maree D5
Janet's Well, Portnockie G5
Kate McNiven's Stone, Monzie F8
Kempock Stone, Gourock D9
Kilchoman Cross B9
Kilhern Well, Kilhern Moss D11
Kincardine O'Neil Old Parish
  Church and Well G6
Kintraw Cairns and Standing Stone
  C8
Kirkton of Aberfoyle E8
Lix Well, Wester Lix E7
Loch Siant Well C5
Maggie Walls Monument,
  Dunning F8
Malsach Well, Knockandy Hill G6
Mine Howe, Tankerness G2
Munlochy Well E5
Museum of Scotland, Edinburgh
  F9
Noltland Castle (HS) F1
North Berwick Auld Kirk G8
Rhymer's Stone Viewpoint, Eildon
  Hills G9
Ring of Brodgar (HS) F2
Skipness Castle (HS) C9
Slot Well and Rumbling Well,
  Barskeoch Hill E11
St Bennet's Well, Navity E5
St Blane's Church, Kingarth (HS)
  D9
St Catherine's Balm Well,
  Edinburgh F9
St Clement's Church, Rodel (HS)
  B5
St Fillan's Chair and Well,
  Dunfillan E8

St Fillan's Church, Aberdour F8
St Fillan's Well, Kilallan D9
St John the Baptist's Well,
   Fodderty E5
St Margaret's Cave, Dunfermline
   F8
St Margaret's Stone, Pitreavie F8
St Mary's Chapel, Crosskirk (HS)
   F3
St Mary's Kirk, Auchindour (HS)
   G6
St Mary's Parish Church,
   Whitekirk G8
St Mary's Well, Culloden E5
St Mary's Well, Elgin F5
St Mary's Well, Orton G5
St Michael's Parish Church,
   Linlithgow F9
St Michael's Well, Williamston G6
St Moluag's Church, Eoropie C3
St Mungo's Well, Glasgow E9
St Ninian's Well, Lamington F9
St Queran's Well, Islesteps F11
St Ronan's Wells Interpretive
   Centre, Innerleithen F9
St Triduana's Well, Edinburgh
   (HS) F9
St Wallach's Well, Dumeath G5
Standing Stone, North Ronaldsay
   G1
Stenton G9
Stones of Stenness (HS) F2
Strontoiller Standing Stone and
   Cairn D7
Tamlane's Well, Carterhaugh
Tarbat Discovery Centre,
   Portmahomack E4
Teampull na Trionaid, Carinish A5
Tigh an Tobar F7
Tobar Bial na Buaidh, Dalvuie D7
Tobar Chaluim Chille, Laiaval A5
Tobar na Bile, Inverliever D8
Tobar na Suil, Luing C8

Tobar nam Buaidh, St Kilda
Tobar nan Dileag, Tullichuil E7
Trumpan Church B5
Up Helly Aa Exhibition, Lerwick
Witch's Stone, Dornoch E4
Witch's Stone, Spott G9

Codes after the place refers to the
   grid reference on the map.

LEGEND

HS   Historic Scotland
NTS   National Trust for Scotland
£   Admission under £3.50
££   Admission £3.50-£5.00
£££   Admission over £5.00

Historic Scotland
Longmore House,
Salisbury Place,
Edinburgh EH9 1SH
Tel: 0131 668 8800
Web: www.historic-scotland.gov.uk

The National Trust for Scotland
Wemyss House,
28 Charlotte Square, Edinburgh
EH2 4ET
Tel: 0844 493 2100
Web: www.nts.org.uk

*Information supplied is for
guidance only: check all details
before setting out on any visit. The
sites listed are a personal selection.
It is not an indication that they
can or should be visited.*

110

Abernethy (HS)
[Map: F8] On A913, 6 miles SE of Perth, Abernethy, Perthshire. (NGR: NO 190165   LR: 58)
There are believed to have been several witchcraft prosecutions at Abernethy, commemorated by the Witch's Cave or Hole, Witch's Road and the Wizard's Stone (reputedly where a local warlock was executed). Twenty-two individuals are said to have been burned on Abernethy Hill. There is a interesting walk (Abernethy Glen Circular Walk) beginning at Kirk Wynd.

  The imposing round tower is all that remains of an important and ancient monastic centre. There are good views from the top of the tower, and a fine carved Pictish stone is located at its base. There is also an interesting museum at School Wynd.
Parking Nearby
Tel: 0131 668 8800 (tower)/
www.museumofabernethy.co.uk (museum)

Applecross
[Map: C5] Off A896, Applecross, 1 mile N of village, Ross-shire. (NGR: NG 713458   LR: 24)
This is the site of an early Christian monastery and place of pilgrimage, founded by Maelrubha in 673. Earth taken from his grave was thought to ensure a safe return from a journey. A holy well [NG 717450], with steps down to it, issues from near the road, west of Applecross House.

  A nearby stone circle is said to have been associated with the sacrifice of bulls, as late as the seventeenth century, a ritual associated with St Maelrubha's feast day (21 April), but probably echoing a much older custom (also see Isle Maree). One of the stones had a hole in the middle of it, but the circle was apparently destroyed by the local minister.

  An eighth-century cross-slab stands by the gate of the church. A nearby ruinous chapel, dating from the fifteenth century, is roofed over by a bush growing up inside the walls.
Parking nearby.
Access at all reasonable times.

Auldearn Church
[Map: F5] Off B9111, 2 miles E of Nairn, Auldearn, Highland. (NGR: NH 919556   LR: 27)

The kirkyard of Auldearn Church is where Isobel Gowdie confessed to being baptised by the cloven-footed Devil, to meeting the King of the Fairies and to flying on a piece of straw, causing illness in children and cattle, and summoning storms. Unusually, she admitted to meeting in a coven of thirteen. She also met the Queen of the Fairies, who was clad in white and brown, on Downie Hill. Isobel was tried in 1662, and probably executed.

The remains of the old church survive beside its eighteenth- and nineteenth-century replacement, and there are some interesting old burial markers.

Access at all reasonable times.

Ballymeanoch Standing Stones
[Map: C8] Off A816, 2 miles S of Kilmartin, Ballymeanoch, Argyll. (NGR: NR 833965   LR: 55)

The remains of a henge stand near a setting of four impressive stones and, parallel to this, two further stones, with the remains of a burial cairn a short distance away. There was formerly also a fallen stone pierced with a hole, which was used for the sealing of contracts, such as handfasting: the two parties would join hands through the hole. This stone has been destroyed, and some of the stones are carved with cup and ring marks.
Parking nearby (Dunchraigaig).
Access at all reasonable times.

Balquhidder Kirk
[Map: E8] Off A84, 14 miles NW of Callendar, Balquhidder Kirkyard, Stirlingshire. (NGR: NN 535209   LR: 57)

Reverend Robert Kirk, author of *The Secret Commonwealth of Elves, Fauns and Fairies* was minister here from 1664 until 1685, when he moved to Aberfoyle. Robert Kirk's bell, dating from the seventeenth century, is kept in the modern church.

St Angus's Stone (Clach Aenais) was 'removed [from the old church] to destroy a superstitious desire that existed among the parishioners to stand or kneel on it during a marriage or baptism'; and was named after Angus, an early saint, and may have been his burial marker.

The old parish church is ruined; and also kept in the modern church is St Angus's Stone.

Rob Roy MacGregor, his wife, and two of his sons are buried here: his memorial stone has a sword roughly carved on it.
Parking nearby
Access at all reasonable times.

Ben Newe
[Map: F6] Off A97, 2 miles NE of Strathdon, Ben Newe,
Aberdeenshire. (NGR: NJ 382143   LR: 37)
The healing well, which is fed by rainwater, is located on the summit of the 1800-feet Ben Newe. Pins, charms and coins were left here (and coins still are).

Braemou Well, Hopeman
[Map: F5] Off B9040, 0.5 miles E of Hopeman, Braemou,
Moray. (NGR: NJ 152699   LR: 28)
The holy and physick (healing) well is a natural spring within a small walled enclosure. It was visited at Beltane and Hallowe'en to protect against the evil eye.

Breadalbane Folklore Centre, Killin
[Map: E7] On A827, Falls of Dochart, Killin, Stirlingshire.
(NGR: NN 573324   LR: 51)
Killin is associated with St Fillan, the early saint, and his famous sacred healing stones. The eight healing stones are shaped like different parts of the body, particularly the heart, body, legs, arms and head. The stones would be doused in water, and the appropriate stone would be rubbed on the afflicted part of the body. They were thought to be particularly effective on 9 January, St Fillan's Day. The top of St Fillan's pastoral

113

staff or crozier is held in the Museum of Scotland.

The folklore centre, which includes a tourist information centre, features displays on St Fillan; the history of local clans, such as the MacLarens, MacNabs, Campbells and MacGregors; and a working water wheel. Information is also available on the natural history and wildlife of the area.

Guided tours by request. Explanatory displays. Gift shop. WC. Disabled access. Induction loop. Car and coach parking. Group concessions. £.

Open early Apr-Oct, daily 10.00-16.00.

Tel: 01567 820254

Web: www.breadalbanefolklorecentre.com

Burghead

[Map: F5] Off B9089, 8 miles NW of Elgin, Burghead, Moray. (NGR: NJ 110690   LR: 28)

Burghead Well was rediscovered in 1809, and is believed to be associated with St Ethan. The subterranean well chamber is hewn out of rock; and a deep tank of water, with a basin and pedestal, is surrounded by a platform and reached down a flight of stone steps.

Burghead is also famous for the 'Burning of the Clavie', an old fire festival when a burning barrel of tar is taken around the streets on 11/12 January. This is to celebrate New Year, and obtaining a piece of the Clavie brings good luck for the rest of the year. The date reflects the old New Year, before the adoption of the Gregorian calendar.

Burghead was an important Pictish stronghold, although it had been used since prehistoric times. Many fine Pictish carvings of bulls were found here, which can now been seen on display in the Burghead Museum, Elgin Museum, the Museum of Scotland in Edinburgh and the British Museum in London. Some impressive earthworks survive, but the fort was mostly destroyed when the village was built.

Parking nearby.

Tel: 01667 460232

114

Callanish (Calanais) Standing Stones (HS)
[Map: B3] Off A858, 14 miles W of Stornoway, Callanish, Lewis. (NGR: NB 213330 LR: 8)
Dating from as early as 5000 years ago, Callanish is one of the most important prehistoric sites in Britain. The main setting, however, is only one part of a complex of single stones, arrangements and circles, perhaps comprising twenty different sites. The whole complex appears to have been aligned to mirror the position of the moon at the summer and winter solstices, as well as at the equinoxes.

The main setting has an avenue of nineteen upright stones, which leads north from a circle of thirteen monoliths. Further rows of stones reach out to the south, east and west; and the tallest stone is over fifteen feet high. A visitor centre features the exhibition 'The Story of the Stones'.
Visitor Centre: Explanatory displays. Gift shop. Tearoom. WC. Disabled access & WC. Parking. £ (visitor centre).
Sites open all year; visitor centre open Apr-Sep, Mon-Sat 10.00-19.00; Oct-Mar, Wed-Sat 10.00-16.00.
Tel: 01851 621422 Web: www.callanishvisitorcentre.co.uk

Carnwath Church
[Map: F9] On A721, 5 miles E of Lanark, W side of Carnwath, Lanarkshire. (NGR: NS 975465 LR: 72)
Margaret Watson, Jean Lachlan and others were tried in 1644 for witchcraft, and confessed that they had met the Devil, described as a black man, on occasions at the cemetery of Carnwath Church and the High Kirk of Lanark. They claimed they had flown on various objects, including a bail of straw, a cat and a thorn tree.

Part of the old church of Carnwath survives alongside a newer building on a different alignment. The remnant was used as a burial aisle for the Somervilles, and houses a sixteenth-century tomb, along with other memorials.
Access at all reasonable times.

Chapel Well, Chapel of Seggat

[Map: G5] Off B992, 5 miles S of Turriff, Chapel of Seggat, Aberdeenshire. (NGR: NJ 727426   LR: 29)

The spring, housed in a dry-stone chamber down a step, was a holy well dedicated St Mary (Our Lady). There was a chapel nearby.

Chapel Wells, Mull of Galloway Farm

[Map: D11] Off B7041, 3.5 miles S of Drummore, Mull of Galloway Farm, Kirkmaiden, Rhinns of Galloway, Dumfries and Galloway. (NGR: NX 144316   LR: 82)

Wells here, which are in natural rock below the high water mark, were associated with the nearby St Medan's or Medana's Chapel. Medana (also known as Modwenna) was renowned for her piety and chastity, and died about 519. She founded several churches in this part of Scotland. Medana has a similar story associated with her as Triduana: her would-be lover would not take no for an answer until she gouged out her own eyes. She was lucky enough to have her eyesight restored, however, by the water from the well: Triduana was less fortunate and remained eyeless.

The wells were visited by ill people on the first Sunday of May, apparently as late as 1940, and offerings left at the chapel. The old parish church of Kirkmaiden, dedicated to St Medana, is nearby [NW 138325]. The well was believed to be especially effective for eye conditions.

Cheese Well, Minch Moor

[Map: F9] Off B709, 3 miles S of Innerleithen, S side of Minchmoor Road, Minch Moor, Borders. (NGR: NT 357336 LR: 73)

The well here, on the south side of the track, was used by travellers to secure a safe passage on the old drove track, described as a 'wild old road', across the somewhat foreboding moor. Offerings of cheese or other food were left to the fairies or other nasty spirits who were believed to inhabit the area

116

and torment travellers. There are two carved stones by the well, one with the legend 'Cheese Well'. Food is still being left here and the track over the moor is now part of the Southern Upland Way.

Accessible at all reasonable times: Southern Upland Way (signposted from Traquair hamlet).

Claypotts Castle (HS)

[Map: F7] Off A92, 3.5 miles E of Dundee, Angus. (NGR: NO 452319 LR: 54)

Claypotts Castle is an unusual Z-plan tower house, and (as well as having a White Lady) the impressive and well-preserved building had a brownie. The brownie eventually left in disgust, casting a malison (or curse) on the place. Claypotts was built by the Strachans, before passing to the Grahams, one of whom was John Graham of Claverhouse of Jacobite fame.

Parking Nearby. £.

Tel to check: 01786 431324.

Colonsay House Gardens

[Map: C8] Off A871, 2 miles N of Scalasaig, Kiloran, Colonsay. (NGR: NR 395968 LR: 61)

In the garden of Colonsay House, which dates from 1722, is Tobar Oran, a round covered well with steps leading down to the water. Beside the well is St Oran's Cross, which is carved with the face of a man and dates from early Christian times. The Big House on Colonsay had a brownie. The rhododendron garden covers some twenty acres, and there are various, more formal, walled gardens plus a natural woodland garden (the woodland garden is open all year, daily).

Lunches and afternoon teas. Shop selling local produce and crafts. Picnic area. Parking. Self-catering accommodation available in Colonsay House (and island cottages).

Open in summer, Wed & Fri only.

Tel: 01951 200211

Web: www.colonsay.org.uk

Craigiehowe Cave
[Map: E5] Off A9 or B9161, 4.5 miles N of Inverness, S side of Munlochy Bay, Craigiehowe, Ross and Cromarty, Highland. (NGR: NH 685522 LR: 26)
At the mouth of the cave is a dripping spring, which was a healing well visited by people to help deafness as well as consumption (tuberculosis). The cave was traditionally used by Finn MacCool or his men.

Dagon Stone, Darvel
[Map: E9] Off A71, 9 miles E of Kilmarnock, Hastings Square, Darvel, Ayrshire. (NGR: NS 563374 LR: 71)
The standing stone, now surmounted by a smaller stone, is known as the Dagon Stone. One ritual was that newly married couples circled the stone for good luck. Dagon was the name of a god of the Philistines, but 'dagone' is also an old Scots word for villain. It is possible that this was one of the sanctuary stones for the church. The stone was moved to Hastings Square in the 1960s.
Access at all reasonable times.

Doon Hill, Aberfoyle
[Map: E8] Off A821, 1 miles SE of Aberfoyle, Doon Hill, Stirlingshire. (NGR: NN 525002 LR: 57)
In a clearing on Doon Hill is a clootie tree, an old Scots pine, known as the Minister's Pine. Reverend Robert Kirk, who was minister of Aberfoyle from 1685 until his death in 1692, wrote *The Secret Commonwealth of Elves, Fauns and Fairies* a year before he died. Kirk was out walking on Doon Hill when he collapsed, and he was buried in the cemetery at Kirkton of Aberfoyle (see separate entry). The story goes, however, that he was actually seized and imprisoned by the fairies on Doon Hill, and is trapped within the Minister's Pine.
Access at all reasonable times: signposted, along with the old kirk, as the 'Fairy Trail'.

Dow Loch, Penpont
[Map: E10] Penpont, Dumfries and Galloway.
Dow or Dubh Loch was believed to be effective in healing many different kinds of diseases, and also reputedly had a water spirit, 'to whom devotees left some part of their dress as an offering'. This later assertion of an 'offering' is probably mistaken: rags and clothing were usually left behind at these sites in an attempt to transfer the disease from the person to the rag, then as the rag rots so the disease improves.

Dunskey Castle
[Map: D11] Off A77, 5.5 miles SW of Stranraer, Dunskey, Portpatrick, Dumfries and Galloway. (NGR: NX 994534 LR: 82)
Set on a windswept and oppressive headland above the sea, Dunskey Castle is a ruinous sixteenth-century tower house of the Adairs. It was at Dunskey that the last abbot of Soulseat Abbey was imprisoned and tortured until he signed over the abbey lands. A brownie also frequented the castle.
Parking Nearby.
View from exterior – climb and walk to castle from Portpatrick: care should be taken.

Dunstaffnage Castle (HS)
[Map: C7] Off A85, 3.5 miles NE of Oban, Dunstaffnage, Argyll. (NGR: NM 882344 LR: 49)
Dunstaffnage Castle, built on a rock on a promontory in the Firth of Lorn, had a gruagach, known as the Ell Maid. Dressed in a green frock, the gruagach would be happy when there was good news to come, but would wail and shriek when death or misfortune was about to strike. It could pass on handicraft skills and teased children staying in the castle, but would also clump about and could make the building shake as if there was an earthquake.

The castle was built by the MacDougalls, and was captured by Robert the Bruce in 1309. Flora MacDonald was briefly

imprisoned here, and there is a fine ruined chapel nearby. *Explanatory panels. Gift shop. WC. Car and coach parking. Group concessions. ££. Joint entry ticket available with Bonawe Iron Furnace.*
Open Apr-Sep, daily 9.30-18.30; Oct, daily 9.30-16.30; Nov-Mar, Sat-Wed 9.30-16.30, closed Thu & Fri; last ticket 30 mins before closing; closed 25/26 Dec and 1/2 Jan. Tel: 01631 562465

Dunvegan Castle
[Map: B5] Off A850, 1 mile N of Dunvegan, Skye. (NGR: NG 247491   LR: 23)
Dunvegan is the home of the famous Fairy Flag, Am Bratach Sith in Gaelic. The flag is much reduced in size (from pieces being removed and kept for luck) and somewhat threadbare and there are many legends about its origins. One account is that it was given to a chief by his fairy wife at their parting. The chief had married his wife thinking she was a mortal woman, but she was only permitted to stay with him for twenty years before she had to return to Fairyland. It is said that they parted at the Fairy Bridge, three miles to the north east, at a meeting of a river and road.

The flag appears to have originated from the Middle East, and has been dated to between 400 and 700 AD, predating the castle by hundreds of years. It was believed to make the marriage of the MacLeods fruitful, when draped on the wedding bed. It was also claimed that it could charm the herrings out of Dunvegan Loch and ensure victory for the clan when it is unfurled. According to accounts it could only be used for the latter three times: the clan have used it twice, at the battles of Glendale in 1490 and Trumpan in 1580. Belief in its power was such that during World War II pilots from the clan carried a picture of the flag with them as a talisman.

Dunvegan Castle stands on what was once an island in Loch Dunvegan to the north of Skye. It has been continuously occupied by the chiefs of MacLeod since 1270, and is still owned by the 29th Chief of MacLeod. There are other family heirlooms, as well as mementoes of Bonnie Prince Charlie and Flora MacDonald, and information about St Kilda.

Info cards in various languages in each of the public rooms. Guides on-hand. Audio-visual theatre. Gift shops. Restaurant. WC. Gardens. Boat trips (££) to seal colony. Dunvegan seal colony. Pedigree Highland cattle fold. Car and coach parking. Group/student/OAP concessions. Holiday cottages available, also wedding venue. £££.

Open Apr-mid Oct, daily 10.00-17.00; other times by appt for groups of 10+; closed 20 Dec-3 Jan.

Tel: 01470 521206

Web: www.dunvegancastle.com

Edinburgh Castle (HS)

[Map: F9] Off A1, in the centre of Edinburgh.
(NGR: NT 252735   LR: 66)

Many people accused of witchcraft, including Janet Douglas, Lady Glamis, were executed on the Castle Hill, at Edinburgh Castle; the site of which is now occupied by the Esplanade. A plaque commemorates some 300 individuals said to have been burned here

Edinburgh Castle was one of the strongest and most important fortresses in Scotland. The oldest building is a small Romanesque chapel of the early 12th century, dedicated to St Margaret, wife of Malcolm Canmore. The castle has a long and eventful history, and only a little of it can be recorded here. It had an English garrison from 1296 until 1313 during the Wars of Independence, when the Scots, led by Thomas Randolph, climbed the rock, surprised the garrison, and retook it. The castle was slighted, but there was an English garrison here again until 1341, when it was retaken by a Scottish force disguised as merchants. In 1566 Mary, Queen of Scots, gave birth to the future James VI in the castle. The Jacobites besieged the castle in both the 1715 and 1745 Risings but unsuccessfully.

The castle is the home of the Scottish crown jewels, the huge fifteenth-century cannon Mons Meg, the National War Museum of Scotland, and the Stone of Destiny – on which the Kings of Scots were inaugurated – and is an interesting complex of buildings with spectacular views over the capital. Scottish War Memorial and Regimental Museum of the Royal Scots.

Explanatory displays. Audio-guide tour. Guided tours. Gift shop. Restaurant. WC. Disabled access. Visitors with a disability can be taken to the top of the castle by a courtesy vehicle; ramps and lift access to Crown Jewels and Stone of Destiny. Car and coach parking (except during Tattoo). £££. Open all year: Apr-Oct, daily 9.30-17.15 (last ticket sold); Nov-Mar, daily 9.30-16.15 (last ticket sold), castle closes 45 mins after last ticket is sold; times may be altered during Tattoo and state occasions; closed 25/26 Dec. Tel: 0131 225 9846

Eildon Hills
[Map: G9] Off A6091, 1 mile SE of Melrose, Eildon, Borders. (NGR: NT 555238   LR: 73)
The Eildon Hills, near Melrose, have many stories associated with them, not least that Thomas the Rhymer disappeared to fairyland here for seven years after meeting the Queen of the Elves at the Eildon Tree (see Rhymer's Stone Viewpoint). The famous wizard, Michael Scott, is also said to have gained his powers in the hills, and to have instructed the famous Evil Lord Soulis of Hermitage Castle.

The summit of Eildon Hill North, the largest of three peaks, was occupied since at least the Bronze Age. Some of the 300 or so houses (represented by house-platforms) date to the late Bronze Age but others are Iron Age. On the west end of the summit are traces of a Roman signal station.

Access at all reasonable times.

Fairy Bridge
[Map: B5] On A850, 3 miles NE of Dunvegan, Skye. *(NGR: NG 278512 LR: 23)*
The Fairy Bridge stands at the meeting of three roads. It is now a stone built bridge and it said to be where the chief of MacLeods parted from his fairy wife, by whom he had had a child. The Fairy Flag, which is preserved at Dunvegan (also see Dunvegan Castle), is claimed to have been given to the chief by his fairy lover.
Parking nearby.
Access at all reasonable times.

Forfar
[Map: G7] Off A926, A929 or A932, 20 West High Street, Forfar, Angus. *(NGR: NO 455506 LR: 54)*
Forfar was the scene of a famous witchcraft prosecution in 1661, involving many suspects, and centred around Helen Guthrie. She implicated many of her acquaintances, and admitted to drunken revelry in the kirkyard of Forfar, desecration of corpses, cannibalism, and with sinking a ship at Carnoustie and destroying a bridge at Cortachy, as well as poisoning one of the baillies. John Kincaid, a witch pricker was used to identify witches, and in all at least nine women were executed by 1662, including Helen herself, and two were banished.

The Meffan Museum in Forfar has displays charting the history of Forfar, including the witch trials. It also houses a collection of Pictish carved stones, all from Kirriemuir, and there is an excellent interactive guide to the stones.
Parking nearby. Explanatory displays. Gift shop. WC.
Disabled access to ground floor only. Car and coach parking nearby. Parties welcome but must book.
Meffan Museum: open all year, Mon-Sat 10.00-17.00; closed Christmas and New Year.
Tel: 01307 464123
Web: www.angus.gov.uk

Glamis Castle

[Map: F7] Off A94, 5.5 miles SW of Forfar, 1 mile N of Glamis village, Angus. (NGR: NO 387481   LR: 54)

Glamis Castle is said to be haunted by the Grey Lady of Glamis, the ghost of Janet Douglas, Lady Glamis, who was burnt for witchcraft by James V. James despised Janet's family – the Douglases – and accused her of trying to murder him using witchcraft and poisoning as part of his revenge against the whole family. The castle is reputed to be one the most haunted sites in Britain, not the least by the ghost of Alexander Lindsay fourth Earl of Crawford, 'Earl Beardie', who is said to haunt a walled-up room where he played cards with the Devil.

   The castle is a hugely impressive and striking fortress, and consists of a greatly extended fourteenth-century keep with later ranges, set in an extensive park. It is a property of the Lyon Earls of Strathmore and Kinghorne.

Collections of historic pictures, porcelain and furniture. Guided tours. Three additional exhibition rooms. Four shops. Licensed restaurant. WC. Picnic area. Play park. Extensive park, pinetum, nature trail and garden. Disabled access to gardens and ground floor; WC. Car and coach parking. Group concessions. £££.

Open mid-Mar-Dec: mid-Mar-Oct, daily 10.00-18.00 (last tour 16.30); Nov-Dec, daily 10.30-16.30 (last tour 15.00); closed 24-26 Dec

Tel: 01307 840393

Web: www.glamis-castle.co.uk

Glamis Well, Church and Pictish Stone

[Map: F7] Off A928, 5.5 miles SW of Forfar, Glamis, Angus. (NGR: NO 386468   LR: 54)

This is an early Christian site and there was a church at Glamis from the twelfth century. A healing well, dedicated to the early saint Fergus, is below the present church [NO 386470], and there was also a cave. A trail, which has been landscaped, leads from the church to the well. Not much remains of an old church except the south transept which was used as the burial vault of the Earls of Strathmore. It has been restored and the rest of the building was replaced by a new church in 1793.

In the adjacent garden of Glamis Manse (across the road from the church) there is a carved Pictish stone [NO 386469] which may have been associated with the healing well. Fragments of other Pictish carved stones are housed in the modern church.

The Angus Folk Museum is located in Glamis and the castle is nearby.

Parking nearby. Sales area nearby.
Church, carved stone and healing well open at all reasonable times.

Glendevon Parish Church
[Map: F8] On A823, 6 miles N of Dollar, 0.5 miles NW of Glendevon village, Clackmannan.
(NGR: NN 980051   LR: 58)
Glendevon churchyard was the site of three meetings with the Devil, or so it was said in the confession of John Brughe. He was prosecuted in 1643, and was accused of desecrating graves and digging up corpses, and causing illness and livestock death. He had been well known as a healer, which may have been what initially got him into trouble with the authorities. Brughe was found guilty and executed on Castle Hill in Edinburgh.

The small church stands in a lovely spot by the River Devon, and the present building dates from the seventeenth century, with later alterations.
Access at all reasonable times.

Hill o' Many Stanes, Mid Clyth (HS)
[Map: F3] Off A9, 4 miles NE of Lybster, Mid Clyth, Caithness, Highland. (NGR: ND 295384   LR: 11)
The Hill o' Many Stanes is a fan-shaped arrangement of over 200 standing stones set in twenty-two rows down the side of the hill. The function of the site is not known, but it may have

been an astronomical observatory. This type of site is only found in northern Scotland and in Brittany in northern France. Access at all reasonable times.

Tel: 01667 460232

Hole Stone, Crouse
[Map: E11] Just E of B7052, 4 miles W of Wigtown, Crouse, Kirkinner, Dumfries and Galloway.
(NGR: NX 365557 LR: 83)
The standing stone is an egg-shaped boulder, about five feet high. It has a hole through it, about two feet from the top. This stone, and another nearby which has gone, were associated with handfasting and marriage ceremonies, and other contracts.

Hole Stone, Dalry
[Map: E10] Off A702, 6 miles W Dalry, Minnygryle, Castlefairn, Dumfries and Galloway.
(NGR: NX 725869 LR: 77)
The three-foot high standing stone had a hole near the top. The stone was associated with handfasting and marriage ceremonies.

Holyrood Park, Edinburgh (HS)
[Map: F9] Off A1, 1 mile E of Edinburgh Castle, Holyrood Park, Edinburgh. (NGR: NT 274734 LR: 66)
The remains of St Anthony's Chapel and St Anthony's Well [NT 275736] are located in Holyrood Park. The well, which has a stone bowl for collecting the water, was a healing well but people also visited it on 1 May (or Beltane) in the hope of improving their looks. The well is now dry, although the water appears to be piped to the St Margaret's Well.

St Margaret's Well [NT 271737] is located near the track to Hunter's Bog opposite Holyrood Palace. The well is housed in a small vaulted building, which is apparently based on the crypt at St Triduana's Well at Restalrig. This building was moved from the present site of St Margaret's House near

Meadowbank in 1860. The site was then used as railway workshops, and the well was rebuilt here.

There was another well in the park, known as St Vining's Well, but the site has not been identified.

Holyrood Park is in the centre of Edinburgh and there are several entrances, including a gate beside Holyrood House. There are a number of small lochs with many birds, including swans and ducks. Visitors can enjoy many walks around the park as well as the excellent views of Edinburgh from the top of Arthur's Seat. There appear to have been fortifications at several locations in the park; there is also evidence of settlements and farming. In the absence of excavation, however, it is very difficult to date these sites but they are likely to have been late Bronze and Iron Age.

Car parking.

Access at all reasonable times. (tel: 0131 556 1761)

House of Dun, Montrose (NTS)

[Map: G7] Off A935, 3 miles NW of Montrose, Angus.
(NGR: NO 667599   LR: 54)

Four members of the Erskine family, associated with the House of Dun, were accused of witchcraft and poisoning in the seventeenth century. They attempted to murder the two young male heirs in a dispute about ownership and three of the siblings – Robert, Isobel and Annas – were executed. The third sister, Helen, was banished to Orkney. One of the two boys, John, died but the other, Alexander, survived. Rather unflattering portraits of those involved can be seen at the house.

An elegant classical mansion, the present House of Dun was built in 1730 by William Adam for David Erskine, Lord Dun.

Explanatory displays. Gift shop. Restaurant. Adventure playground. Fine plasterwork and a collection of portraits, furniture and porcelain. Walled garden and handloom weaving workshop. Woodland walk. Disabled access to ground floor and basement and WC. Info in Braille. £££.

House open Apr-Jun & Sep-Oct, Wed-Sun 12.00-17.00;

Jul & Aug, daily 11.00-17.00; restaurant same dates, daily 11.00-18.00; garden and grounds open all year, daily 9.30-sunset; house closed some days for private functions.
Tel: 0844 493 2144

Inchadney
[Map: E7] Off A827, 5 miles W of Aberfeldy, Inchadney, Kenmore, Perthshire. (NGR: NN 787472   LR: 51)
The well here, which is signposted 'Holy Well', is topped by a quartz stone. Coins and pins, which were left as offerings, as well as a stone cup, were found here and are now held by the Museum of Scotland. Little remains of a old church and burial ground.

Isle Maree, Loch Maree
[Map: D5] Off A832, 9 miles NW of Kinlochewe, Loch Maree, Highland. (NGR: NG 931724   LR: 19)
There is a healing well on an island in Loch Maree, which was used for curing lunacy as late as the nineteenth century. Coins and nails, as well as pieces of cloth and rag, were hammered into the trunk of a nearby oak tree. Oak trees were believed to be sacred, and may have reflected a pre-Christian belief.
  Loch Maree, one of the most beautiful lochs in Scotland, is also the site of a chapel and remains of a burial ground, which are believed to have been founded by St Maelrubha, although there also appear to have been older pagan traditions associated with the site. Bulls were sacrificed here, as they were at Applecross, and later the custom was associated with St Maelrubha's day, 21 April.

Janet's Well, Portnockie
[Map: G5] Off A942, SE of Portnockie, Cruats, Moray. (NGR: NJ 496682   LR: 28)
The well is said to be named after a 'mad woman' – presumably called Janet – who lived in a cave nearby, although it also bears the legend 'Jenny's Well'. A spring flows into a semi-circular

well and pins and other small offerings were left here. By the beginning of the nineteenth century the well was visited on 1 May or Beltane.

Kate McNiven's Stone, Monzie
[Map: F8] Off A822, 2 miles N of Crieff, drive to Monzie Castle, Perthshire. (NGR: NN 840243   LR: 58)
The standing stone is said to mark the site of Kate McNiven or MacNieven's, sometimes known as the Witch of Monzie, execution. The story goes that she was put in a barrel and rolled down what is now known as Kate MacNieven's Craig on the north side of the Knock of Crieff before being burnt. Kate had been nurse to the Grahams of Inchbrackie, and was accused of witchcraft, including turning herself into a bee. Graham of Inchbrackie tried to save her to no avail, but as she was about to die it is said that she spat a bead from her necklace into his hand. The bead – a blue sapphire – was turned into a ring and it was believed that the ring would keep the family and lands secure. She did, however, curse the laird of Monzie, although whether this worked or not is not known. MacNiven or Nic Niven was also believed to be the name of the Queen of Fairies.

Indeed it is not clear whether Kate MacNiven was a real person or is a conflation of stories. There do not appear to be any contemporary records of her execution at or near Crieff, and dates for her unpleasant death are variously given as 1563, 1615 and 1715.

Ask permission from lodge of Monzie Castle before visiting.

Kempock Stone, Gourock
[Map: D9] Off A770, 2.5 miles W of Greenock, Kempock Point, Gourock, Renfrewshire. (NGR: NS 243780   LR: 63)
This six-feet tall stone is known as the Kempock Stone, or Granny Kempock Stone, as it bears some resemblance to a cloaked and hooded old women. Fishermen performed rituals to try to ensure good weather and fair winds, as well as a good

catch of fish, using the stone. They would walk around the stone seven times, carrying a basket of sand. The ritual was used for good luck by betrothed and newly married couples.

In 1662 several women, including the eighteen-year-old Mary Lamont (or Lawmont), were accused of trying to throw the stone into the Clyde (to destroy boats and ships), which would have been some feat in itself, along with using magic to steal milk. Mary also confessed that she had intercourse several times with the Devil (who appeared as a large brown dog), and he had left marks on her by nipping her side. She and several others were accused of witchcraft and apparently executed.

Parking nearby

Access at all reasonable times.

Kilchoman Cross

[Map: B9] Off B8018, 3 miles NW of Bruichladdich, Kilchoman, Islay. (NGR: NR 214631 LR: 60)

The Kilchoman Cross is an eight-foot-high disc-headed cross, which was carved about 1500. It is located in the burial ground of the church and there is a depiction of the Crucifixion on one side, as well as other figures including a horseman and knotwork decoration. There are cups and a stone at the base. According to accounts wishes would be granted if an individual turned the stone in the holes in the correct direction – towards the sun. There are several other carved grave slabs nearby, as well as a stone known as the Sanctuary Cross.

Parking nearby.

Access at all reasonable times.

Kilhern Well, Kilhern Moss

[Map: D11] Off A85, 3.5 miles N of Glenluce, Kilhern Moss, Dumfries and Galloway. (NGR: NX 201642 LR: 82)

The well is located near the Caves of Kilhern. It is a mineral and chalybeate spring, which may have accounted for its healing powers. Small offerings were left at the well, and objects are still found occasionally.

Kincardine O'Neil Old Parish Church and Well

[Map: G6] About 7 miles W of Banchory, just S of A93,
Kincardine O'Neil, Aberdeenshire. (NGR: NO 593995
LR: 44)

St Erchan's, or Erchard's, well stands across the road from the church at Kincardine O'Neil. It is now enclosed in a small building of 1858, although there is no longer any water. The site is associated with St Erchan or Erchard, an early saint, whose festival day was 24 August. There are the remains of a older church, which formerly had a two-storey hospice at one end. There is also a fourteenth-century moulded doorway, and as well as interesting old burial markers. Kincardine O' Neill is known as 'Kinker' by the locals.

Parking nearby.

Access at all reasonable times.

Kintraw Cairns and Standing Stone

[Map: C8] On A816, 4 miles N of Kilmartin, Kintraw,
Argyll. (NGR: NM 830050   LR: 55)

Kintraw Cairns and Standing Stone include a large cairn, a small cairn and a single standing stone. The site has been interpreted as marking the sunset at the mid-winter solstice as the sun set through a notch in the Paps of Jura. The stone was moved to a different alignment when it was re-erected after falling down.

Kirkton of Aberfoyle

[Map: E8] Off A821, 0.5 miles SE of Aberfoyle, Kirkton,
Stirlingshire. (NGR: NN 518005   LR: 57)

The memorial to Reverend Robert Kirk, who died in 1692, is located here. Kirk was minister at Aberfoyle from 1685, and among other works, wrote *The Secret Commonwealth of Elves, Fauns and Fairies* in 1691. He died suddenly on 4 May 1692 while out walking on the Doon Hill. Although he was buried here the story goes that his mortal body was then seized by the fairies, and he is imprisoned in the hill or in an old Scots pine tree that grows on it. Also see entry on Doon Hill. Access at all reasonable times: the old kirk and Doon Hill are both on the signposted 'Fairy Trail'.

Lix Well, Wester Lix

[Map: E7] Off A85, 3 miles SW of Killin, Wester Lix, Stirlingshire. (NGR: NN 545295 LR: 51)
A spring here is enclosed within a wall. It was renowned as a holy and healing well and offerings of quartz pebbles were left here on Beltane (1 May).

Loch Siant Well

[Map: C5] Off A855, 5.5 miles NE of Uig, Digg, Skye. (NGR: NG 471699 LR: 23)
Loch Siant Well was once the most celebrated well on Skye. A spring issues from a bank near Loch Siant and the well is enclosed by stones. It was believed to be a wishing and healing well and rags, pins and coloured threads were left here. According to accounts people would circle the well three times, going sunwise from east to west. They would then drink some of the water, and leave behind a small offering: rags, coins or threads. The site has no recorded dedication, and one story is that there was a grove of sacred oak trees here, perhaps an echo of Druidical custom. No twigs or branches were ever cut from the copse.

Maggie Walls Monument, Dunning

[Map: F8] On B8062, 4 miles E of Auchterarder, 1 mile W of Dunning, Perthshire. (NGR: NO 006141 LR: 58)
The monument, which consists of a rough plinth and a cross, is believed to commemorate the burning of Maggie Walls, a reputed witch, in 1657. Although several people from the Dunning area were accused of witchcraft there is no mention of a Margaret Walls or Wallace, so the name may be apocryphal and used to represent those who were executed rather than one particular person. The writing is regularly renewed and

flowers are often left here. Maggie is said to have been the last person accused of witchcraft to be burnt alive, but it was common practice to throttle those found guilty before torching them.

Car and coach parking.
Access at all reasonable times.

Malsach Well, Knockandy Hill
[Map: G6] Off B9002, 5.5 miles SE of Huntly, NE of Knockandy Hill, Malsach, Aberdeenshire.
(NGR: NJ 554318   LR: 37)
The healing well here was used by women to restore fertility, and was believed to be able to cure other illnesses in both humans and animals. The spring is a mineral well, and buttons, small coins and pieces of cloth were left as offerings.

Mine Howe, Tankerness
[Map: G2] Off A960, 5 miles SE of Kirkwall, Veltigar Farm, Tankerness, Orkney. (NGR: HY 511060   LR: 6)
Built into a massive mound is an underground shaft, that appears to date from the Iron Age, with two flights descending twenty-nine steps. There are two galleries on the way, and at the bottom is a corbelled-out chamber. It bears some resemblance to a well, but its exact purpose remains a mystery. Mine Howe was excavated by Time Team.
Parking nearby. £.
Opening: tel 01856 861209 to confirm.

Munlochy Well
[Map: E5] Just S of A832, 5 miles N of Inverness, 0.5 miles NW of Munlochy, Hill o' Hirdie, Black Isle, Highland.
(NGR: NH 641537   LR: 26)
A strange and somewhat perplexing place, the clootie well here is still in use, and the trees and fence around the well are festooned with rags, pieces of clothing, football shirts, shoes and other items. The well was dedicated to St Curitan or

Boniface, an eighth-century saint who was active among the Picts. To have a wish granted, it is said, a small amount of well water must be spilt on the ground three times, a rag tied on a nearby tree, the sign of the cross made, then a drink of water is taken from the well. Anyone removing a rag from the well will be afflicted by the misfortunes of the person who put it there.

Parking on verge: care should be taken as busy road.
Access at all reasonable times.

Museum of Scotland, Edinburgh
[Map: F9] Chambers Street, Edinburgh.
(NGR: NT 256732   LR: 66)
The Museum of Scotland (part of the National Museums of Scotland) displays and holds extensive collections of Scotland's history, land and people. This includes material related to the decorative arts, natural history, science and technology, working life and geology. There is a permanent exhibition and the museum also has a programme of special exhibitions, films, lectures and concerts, which take place throughout the year.

  Items of particular interest include the Monymusk Reliquary, the crozier of St Fillan, the Clach Dearg, Ballochyle Brooch, examples of elfshot, molucca or molluka beans and Barbreck's Bone.

Museum. Multi-media study room. Gift shop. Audio guides.
Tearooms. Roof-top restaurant. WC. Disabled access & WC.
Parking nearby.
Open all year: daily, 10.00-17.00
Tel: 0131 225 7534
Web: www.nms.ac.uk

Noltland Castle (HS)
[Map: F1] Off B9066, NE side of island of Westray, Orkney.
(NGR: HY 430487   LR: 5)
Noltland Castle is a large ruined sixteenth-century Z-plan tower house, which was associated with a brownie. A strong

and grim stronghold, the present castle was built by Gilbert Balfour, who was Master of the Household to Mary, Queen of Scots. He had been involved in the murders of Cardinal Beaton in 1546, for which he was imprisoned, and Lord Darnley in 1567; he was eventually executed in Sweden.
Open in summer: check dates and times.
Tel: 01856 872044 (or Skara Brae 01856 841815).

North Berwick Auld Kirk
[Map: G8] Off A198, N of North Berwick, by the Seabird Centre, East Lothian. (NGR: NT 554856   LR: 66)
The Auld Kirk is reputedly the place where 200 witches met on a stormy Hallowe'en in 1590, having flown here in sieves, and attempted to sink the ship in which James VI and his new bride Anne of Denmark were returning to Scotland. The Devil had appeared in the guise of a black man. Or so the story goes. Geillis Duncan, who had gained a reputation as a healer, was tortured by her employer into confessing that she was a witch and she went on to implicate many others, including Francis Stewart, Earl of Bothwell. Geillis and many of her alleged accomplices were executed after a trial in which James VI was heavily involved. Bothwell was himself tried in 1593 and, although found not guilty, was soon exiled.

Located by the sea, much of the Auld Kirk, which was once a substantial aisled building dedicated to St Andrew, has been washed away over the years, but the north porch survives. The Scottish Seabird Centre is nearby.
Access at all reasonable times.

Rhymer's Stone Viewpoint, Eildon Hills
[Map: G9] On Old Bogle Burn Road, the old road between Melrose and Newtown St Boswells, Borders.
The stone here is said to mark the spot of the Eildon Tree, where Thomas the Rhymer or True Thomas, Thomas Learmonth of Ercildoune, met the Queen of the Elves, in the thirteenth century. It is claimed that Thomas spent seven years

in the land of the fairies, and when he returned he had the power of prophecy – many of his prophecies are said to have come true. He later disappeared: presumably he had to return to fairyland!

Access at all reasonable times.

Ring of Brodgar (HS)

[Map: F2] On B9055, 5 miles NE of Stromness, Orkney.
(NGR: HY 294134 LR: 6)

This is the most impressive stone circle in Scotland: thirty-six stones out of an original total of sixty remain, some up to fifteen feet high. The site is surrounded by a ditch, making this a henge monument, which was originally up to ten feet deep and thirty feet across. It is crossed by two causeways. The circle is part of a larger ritual complex, which includes Maes Howe and the Stones of Stenness.

A Norse visitor to the site has carved runes and a cross on one of the broken stones in the northern section of the circle.
Car and coach parking.
Access at all reasonable times.
Tel: 01856 841815 (Skara Brae)

Skipness Castle (HS)

[Map: C9] Off B8001, 7 miles S of Tarbert, Skipness, Argyll.
(NGR: NR 907577 LR: 62)

There are stories of a brownie (or gruagach) at Skipness, described as a small woman clad in green with golden hair. The castle is an impressive ruinous stronghold, consisting of a courtyard with a tower house and ranges of buildings, while a later mansion, which replaced the castle, stands nearby.

The first castle was probably built by the MacSweens around 1247, and it was held by the MacDonalds, the Forresters and the Campbells.
Explanatory boards. Car parking.
Access at all reasonable times: short walk to castle.

Slot Well and Rumbling Well, Barskeoch Hill

[Map: E11] Off A745, 0.5 miles NW of Dalbeattie, Barskeoch Hill, Buittle, Dumfries and Galloway.
(NGR: NX 813616   LR: 84)

There are two wells on Barskeoch Hill. One is the Slot Well, which was visited in the seventeenth century by people wanting to cure their ill cattle of connoch or cattle plague. They left behind the bands and shackles used to tether the beasts. The well is now overgrown but still has a flow of water.

Nearby there is another healing well known as the Rumbling Well. It is at the north-east end of Dalbeattie Reservoir and was a clootie well, although other items, including coins, were also left here.

St Bennet's Well, Navity

[Map: E5] Off A832, 1.5 miles S of Cromarty, Navity, Ross and Cromarty, Highland. (NGR: NH 791651   LR: 21)

St Bennet's Well, a healing and clootie well, is located near the sea. It was still being used in 1935 and may still be now. Although there was a chapel nearby, little or nothing of this building survives.

St Blane's Church, Kingarth (HS)

[Map: D9] Off A844, 2 miles S of Kingarth, Bute. (NGR: NS 094535   LR: 63)

There is a holy and wishing well near the ruins of the fine twelfth-century chapel in a picturesque and peaceful location on Bute. There are some remains of the sixth-century monastery, founded by St Blane, who was born on Bute and who is also associated with Dunblane. The chapel and other remains are enclosed by a wall, and the burial ground, which was apparently divided into separate areas for men and women, has some interesting markers.

Parking.

Access at all reasonable times.

St Catherine's Balm Well, Edinburgh
[Map: F9] Off A701, 3.5 miles SE of Edinburgh Castle, Howdenhall Road, Liberton, Edinburgh.
(NGR: NT 272684   LR: 66)
St Catherine's Balm Well (or Oily Well), dedicated to St Catherine of Alexandria, was a healing well used for eczema, skin conditions and even leprosy. The spring issues through oil shale, and a black tarry substance floats on the surface and coats the inside of the well. The well is in the grounds of Balmwell House.

There are stories that Liberton got its name from a leper colony here, but this is far from certain.

The well was patronised by a number of Scottish monarchs. One story is that the well sprang from a drop of holy oil which was being brought from the Holy Land to Queen Margaret, who was later made a saint. James IV visited in 1504 and James VI had a wellhouse built but this was destroyed by Cromwell's forces in 1650. It was later restored in 1889, and the waters were still being used for eczema as least as late as 1910.

St Clement's Church, Rodel (HS)
[Map: B5] On A859, 2.5 miles SE of Leverburgh, Rodel, S of Harris. (NGR: NG 047833   LR: 18)
Several, apparently older carvings adorn the outside of this sixteenth-century cross-shaped church dedicated to St Clement. One of these is a Sheila na Gig, which is very sexually suggestive and believed to be a fertility symbol, found on the outside of the south wall of the tower.

Another Sheila can be found at the nunnery on Iona, and there are many examples in Ireland.

The fine church has a strong square tower at one end, and inside is the splendid carved tomb of Alasdair Crotach MacLeod, who built much of Dunvegan Castle on the Isle of Skye, which was also a property of the clan.
Parking nearby.
Access at all reasonable times.

St Fillan's Chair and Well, Dunfillan
[Map: E8] Off A85, 3.5 miles W of Comrie, St Fillans, Dunfillan, Perthshire. (NGR: NN 709229   LR: 51)
The conical hill of Dunfillan is crowned by a stone known as St Fillan's Chair. It was from here that Fillan is said to have blessed the surrounding lands, and the chair was used in healing rituals, particularly for rheumatism. The sufferer would sit in the chair and be then be dragged back down the hill by their ankles, which would certainly be enough to make someone forget about their bad back. The chair was visited on 1 May (Beltane) and 1 August (Lugnasad or Lammas). There was a healing well and chapel also dedicated to St Fillan. The ruins of the rectangular chapel survive near Wester Dundurn [NN 704237].

St Fillan's Church, Aberdour
[Map: F8] Off A921, 6.5 miles SW of Kirkcaldy, Aberdour, Fife. (NGR: NT 194856   LR: 66)
Near the impressive ruins of the castle, St Fillan's Church stands in a picturesque spot in the attractive village of Aberdour. Near the church, but now in a private garden, was a healing well, which was said to be effective for eye conditions. The well is now covered and drained.

  The church, dedicated to St Fillan, dates from the twelfth century and is a good example of Romanesque architecture. It fell into disrepair but was restored in 1925. It was a place of pilgrimage, although some unkind people might suggest this was to cash in on pilgrims going from Dunfermline to St Andrews.
Open all year.

St Fillan's Well, Kilallan
[Map: D9] Off A761, 1.5 miles E of Kilmacolm, Kilallan, Renfrewshire. (NGR: NS 384690   LR: 63)
St Fillan's Well was a clootie well. Sick children were bathed here and the well was used until the end of the seventeenth

century when the local minister had it filled in. There is an old church nearby [NS 382689] and the spring is now used by livestock.

St John the Baptist's Well, Fodderty
[Map: E5] Off A834, 2 miles W of Dingwall, Fodderty, Ross and Cromarty, Highland. (NGR: NH 514588 LR: 26)
This spring was used as a healing well particularly for mental illnesses; threads and ribbons were left tied to a nearby bush. There was a chapel and large burial ground nearby.

St Margaret's Cave, Dunfermline
[Map: F8] Off A994, Bruce Street car park, Dunfermline. (NGR: NT 087873 LR: 65)
Margaret, wife of Malcolm Canmore, had particular associations with Dunfermline. The cave here was her personal retreat and later became a place of pilgrimage. It is now underneath a car park but can be reached down a stairway and tunnel, which has display panels about Margaret and the cave. The picturesque church and ruins of Dunfermline Abbey and Palace, are nearby.
Explanatory displays. Gift shop. Car and coach parking.
Open Apr-Sep, daily 11.00-16.00.
Tel: 01383 722935(Pittencrieff House Museum)

St Margaret's Stone, Pitreavie
[Map: F8] By A823, 2 miles S of Dunfermline Abbey, 0.5 miles W of Pitreavie, Fife. (NGR: NT 109850 LR: 65)
The large stone here is associated with St Margaret and was visited by women who hoped to conceive or sought a successful birth. The eight-foot high stone is said to mark the resting place of St Margaret when she journeyed between Queensferry and Dunfermline.

Margaret had eight successful pregnancies and probably needed to rest quite a few times on her travels!
Access at all reasonable times.

St Mary's Chapel, Crosskirk (HS)
[Map: F3] Off A836, 6 miles NW of Thurso, Crosskirk,
Caithness. (NGR: ND 024700 LR: 12)
To the south of this chapel there is a healing well, dedicated
to St Mary. The simple dry-stone chapel, possibly built in the
twelfth century, is roofless but the walls are complete. The
building probably had a thatched roof.
Parking nearby.
Access at all reasonable times – may be muddy.
Tel: 01667 460232

St Mary's Kirk, Auchindour (HS)
[Map: G6] Off A97, 8 miles NW of Alford, near Lumsden,
Aberdeenshire. (NGR: NJ 477244 LR: 37)
St Mary's Well, which was used for healing and particularly
toothache is located about 100 yards to the west of the ruinous
shell of a medieval parish church. The remains of the church
include a Romanesque doorway and fourteenth-century
sacrament house.
Parking nearby.
Access to church at all reasonable times: keys available
locally.
Tel: 01667 460232

St Mary's Parish Church, Whitekirk
[Map: G8] On A198, 3.5 miles SE of North Berwick,
Whitekirk, East Lothian. (NGR: NT 596815 LR: 67)
There was an extremely popular well here, which had many
famous visitors and patrons. Whitekirk was recognised as a
place of pilgrimage from around 1295 after Agnes, Countess
of Dunbar, was healed at the well [NT 598817?]. The well
apparently dried up around 1830, and its exact location is
uncertain
   The number of miracles which occurred at the well was so
great that a shrine was built in 1309 and dedicated to St Mary.

It was visited by Aeneas Sylvius Piccolomini, later known as Pope Pious II. He made a pilgrimage to the well in 1435 after being saved from a storm; he walked barefoot from Dunbar to Whitekirk. A fresco in the chapter house of Sienna Cathedral records his visit.

James I placed the site under his protection at the beginning of the fifteenth century and ordered the building of pilgrims' hostels. It was recorded that 15,000 pilgrims visited in 1413. James IV visited but his son James V granted the hostels to one of his favourites Oliver Sinclair, who had them demolished or remodelled into a dwelling.

The fine cruciform church dates from the twelfth century and it has a sixteenth-century tower. Although it was burned by suffragettes in 1914, it was later restored.

Sales area. WC. Parking nearby.

Church: open daily.

St Mary's Well, Culloden

[Map: E5] Off B9006, 3.5 miles E of Inverness, Culloden, Highland. (NGR: NH 723452   LR: 27)

The spring here, dedicated to St Mary, flows into a stone basin. It is enclosed by a wall and is also known as Tobar na h-Oige or 'well of youth'. It is a healing and clootie well, and rags and other items were, and are still being, left on surrounding trees. The well is located in a forestry plantation and is accessible by a forest trail.

Car parking.

Access at all reasonable times: on Forestry Commission land (Yellow Trail).

St Mary's Well, Elgin

[Map: F5] By A96, W side of Elgin, Moray.
(NGR: NJ 208627   LR: 28)

A stone-line well, dedicated to St Mary, is at the base of a wall in Elgin. At one time it had a wide reputation as a healing well and people visited it from many parts of Scotland.

St Mary's Well, Orton

[Map: F5] Off B905, 2 miles S of Fochabers, 0.5 miles E of Inchberry, Orton, Moray. (NGR: NJ 324552   LR: 28)

A spring here is piped into a stone trough, and is walled in stone with a pointed canopy mounted by a small cross. The well is located on the outside of the wall surrounding the burial ground.

  This was a healing well, dedicated to St Mary, and was especially visited on the first Sunday in May and at Lugnasad (1 August). The water was believed to be especially beneficial for whooping cough, painful joints and sore eyes. There were apparently many people still visiting the well in 1914, and the tradition was revived in 1938. The reputation of the well was such that at one time pilgrims would come here from as far afield as the Western Isles.

  There was a chapel nearby, dedicated to St Mary but this has been replaced by a mausoleum of the Duff family and the churchyard is used as a private burial ground.

St Michael's Parish Church, Linlithgow

[Map: F9] Off M9, Kirkgate, Linlithgow, West Lothian. (NGR: NT 003773   LR: 65)

St Michael's Well [NT 004771], is near Linlithgow Palace. It is now in a stone building, which has a rough depiction of the saint and bears the legend 'St Michael is Kinde to Strangers'.

  The church of St Michael was founded in 1242 on the site of an earlier church. Most of the building dates from the fifteenth century, although it now has a modern steeple. The palace and church was associated with the Stewart monarchs, particularly James IV and James V.

Guided tours by arrangement. Explanatory displays. Gift shop. Picnic area. Car and coach parking.

Open May-Sep, daily 10.00-16.00; Oct-Apr, Mon-Fri 10.00-13.00.

Tel: 01506 842188

Web: www.stmichaelsparish.org.uk

St Michael's Well, Williamston

[Map: G6] Off A96, 0.5 miles S of Kirkton of Culsalmond, Williamston, Aberdeenshire. (NGR: NJ 650317 LR: 29)
The well here, which was dedicated to St Michael, is housed in a small domed building. It was used to cure illnesses and was usually visited on the first Sunday in May.

St Moluag's Church, Eoropie (Eoropaidh)

[Map: C3] Off B8014 or B8013, 26 miles N of Stornoway, Eorrapaidh, Lewis. (NGR: NB 519652 LR: 8)
There was a well and chapel near the church at Eoropie, which is dedicated to St Moluag or St Olaf. The well, however, was dedicated to St Ronan, and was used as a cure for madness. Sufferers would be walked seven times around the church, and water from the well was sprinkled on them. The sufferer was then left by the altar, and if they slept well it was believed that they would be cured. The church was also associated with 'hallow-tide sacrifices', probably a fertility rite, to the sea-god Shony, which continued to the end of the seventeenth century, well after the Reformation.

There was probably a Christian settlement here from the sixth century; the present church dates from the twelfth century. The church has round arched windows and door. An adjoining chapel only has a squint – or viewing hole – into the main church and it may have been used by lepers.
Parking nearby.
Open Easter-Sep during daylight hours: short walk - path may be muddy.
Web: www.saintmoluag.com

St Mungo's Well, Glasgow

[Map: E9] Off A8, Gallowgate. (NGR: NS 599647 LR: 64)
This well is also known as St Kentigern's Well as Kentigern was another name for Mungo. It is housed in a low round building and a plaque bears the legend: 'Ancient Well of Little St Mungo'. There was a chapel nearby but this is gone.

St Ninian's Well, Lamington
[Map: F9] Off A702, 5 miles SW of Biggar, Lamington, Lanarkshire. (NGR: NS 984305   LR: 72)
The healing well here, dedicated to St Ninian, is set in a stone-lined basin. An iron ring had a drinking cup attached to it.

St Queran's Well, Islesteps
[Map: F11] Off A710, 2.5 miles SW of Dumfries, Troqueer, Dumfries and Galloway. (NGR: NX 956722   LR: 84)
The clootie well here is dedicated to St Queran, a ninth-century Scottish saint. The water was used for healing, and was particularly effective on women and children. When it was cleared out in 1870 hundreds of coins were found in the water. It is still visited today and items including pins, cloths and ribbons are tied to nearby trees and bushes.
Parking nearby.
Access at all reasonable times: walk to well.

St Ronan's Wells Interpretive Centre, Innerleithen
[Map: F9] Off A72, Wells Brae, Innerleithen, Borders. (NGR: NT 328372   LR: 73)
St Ronan's Well, also known as the 'Dow-well', is an old healing well. In the nineteenth century it was recorded as being used for 'ophthalmic, scorbutic, bilious and dyspeptic complaints'. The water can still be tasted although there are no claims about its curative powers. The site was visited by Sir Walter Scott and used in one of his novels.

  The interpretive centre features memorabilia related to Scott, and also has information and photographs about the local Cleikum ceremony and the St Ronan's Border Games.
Explanatory displays. Gift shop. Tea room on Edwardian verandah. Picnic area. WC. Disabled access. Parking.
Open Apr-Oct, daily: Mon-Fri 10.00-13.00 & 14.00-17.00, Sat-Sun 14.00-17.00.
Tel: 01896 833583

St Triduana's Well, Edinburgh (HS)
[Map: F9] On Restalrig Road South, to E of Edinburgh.
(NGR: NT 282745   LR: 66)
There is an extremely unusual hexagonal vaulted chamber, adjacent to the present church, known as St Triduana's Chapel or Well. It is comprised of the lower parts of a two-storey building, and water still flows from a spring here under the floor. Requests to use the water are still being received today.

Triduana's shrines were supposed to help blindness and other eye complaints and conditions. Triduana was an early convert to Christianity who was the object of desire of a Pagan prince. The prince particularly admired Triduana's eyes and, instead of being forced to marry him, it is said that Triduana plucked out her own eyes and presented them to him on a thorned branch.

There is a similar story attached to St Medana, (although her eyesight was restored; Triduana's was not) as well as other examples from Ireland and the Continent.

The church, which is dedicated to St Mary and The Trinity, was founded as a collegiate establishment by James III in the 1460s, although it is a much older site. There is also an interesting kirkyard.
Parking nearby.
Contact St Margaret's Parish Church, Restalrig - tel: 0131 554 7400   Web: www.stmargarets-restalrig.com

St Wallach's Well, Dumeath
[Map: G5] Off A920, 6 miles W of Huntly, Dumeath, Glass, Aberdeenshire. (NGR: NJ 424371   LR: 28)
St Wallach's Well is 100 yards east of the cemetery of Walla Kirk, although the water now issues from further down the bank. Other sites associated with Wallach are the Wallach's Pot, near the footbridge, and Bath, a trough which is 400 yards down the river Deveron. All three were used in healing rituals, and the bath was particularly useful for sick children. Rags were left here, and pins were left in a holed stone. The

well was still being used in the nineteenth century. In 1607 several people were reprimanded for visiting the well.

There was a church here, but nothing remains except mounds in the burial ground.

Standing Stone, North Ronaldsay
[Map: G1] Off unlisted road, Holland, SW side of North Ronaldsay, Orkney. (NGR: HY 752529 LR: 5)

The standing stone here is over thirteen feet high. It has a small hole through it some six feet above the ground and the stone was used as a meeting place on New Year's Day.

Stenton
[Map: G9] On B6370, 5 miles SW of Dunbar, Stenton, East Lothian. (NGR: NT 633743 LR: 66)

The Cardinal's Hat, a rood well dating from the fourteenth century, is housed in small chamber resembling a cardinal's hat, hence the name. It is located in the picturesque and peaceful village of Stenton. Nearby is the Wool Stone, which stands on the green. It was formerly used for weighing wool at Stenton Fair.

There is also an old doocot, as well as the tower and ruins of a sixteenth-century church, as well as several interesting memorials in the burial ground.

Car parking.

Access at all reasonable times.

Stones of Stenness (HS)
[Map: F2] On B9055, 5 miles NE of Stromness, Stenness, Orkney. (NGR: HY 306126 LR: 6)

Only four stones out of the original twelve remain in this circle. It is surrounded by a ditch, which is over seven feet deep and was crossed by one causeway.

The Stone of Odin was one of the group, and was located some 150 yards to the north. It was about eight feet high, with a hole through it some five feet or so from the ground. It was used by couples during handfasting ceremonies; later they could be divorced by leaving Stenness Church by different doors. The stone continued to be visited by many people, particularly on New Year's Day, into the nineteenth century. These visitors left behind offerings of bread, cheese, stones or rags, which annoyed the local farmer. Eventually he was so irritated that he destroyed the stone in 1814.

The site was excavated in the 1970s, and a stone setting was uncovered in the centre of the circle. Animal bones that were found in the ditch were interpreted as the remains of feasting or sacrifice at the henge.

Car and coach parking.
Access at all reasonable times.
Tel: 01856 841815 (Skara Brae)

Strontoiller Standing Stone and Cairn
[Map: D7] Off A816, 3 miles E of Oban, S of Strontoiller, Argyll. (NGR: NM 907289 LR: 49)
The impressive standing stone at Strontoiller is a rough-cut pillar, standing some thirteen feet high, which was used in healing rituals. It is said to mark the grave of Diarmid, the mythical hero. The adjacent cairn was excavated, and some cremated bone was found. Quartz chips and pebbles were found under the kerbstones: quartz is often associated with burial sites in the west.

Tamlane's Well, Carterhaugh
[Map: G9] By B7039, 2 miles SW of Selkirk, Carterhaugh, Borders. (NGR: NT 437268 LR: 73)
Beside the road there was a well that has been filled in. It was associated with the old ballad *Tam Lin*. Tam, reputedly the son of Thomas Randolph, Earl of Moray, was imprisoned in fairyland until freed by the heroine of the ballad. The well has the legend 'Tamlane's Well'.
Access at all reasonable times.

Tarbat Discovery Centre, Portmahomack
[Map: E4] Off B9165, 8 miles E of Tain, Tarbatness Road,
Portmahomack, Ross and Cromarty, Highland.
(NGR: NH 915845 LR: 21)
At the entrance to the church of St Colman, which now houses
the Discovery Centre, is a rectangular baptismal well. The water
was said to have been blessed by St Rule when he drank some
of the water and threw in a piece of the sacred cross.

The well was used to baptise the eldest sons of the Earls of
Cromartie, the first time being at the instigation of a local
'witch' Kirsty Bheag. This is a very interesting combination
of Christian and non-Christian 'magical' traditions.

The Discovery Centre has displays on one of the largest on-
going archaeological digs in Europe, and information on the
Picts.

Carvings which have been found at the site include cattle
licking their new-born calf, a wild boar, and a dragon with a
serpent head on its tail. The centre features a video on the
Picts of Easter Ross.

Guided tours of the archaeological dig are available when it
is in progress.
Explanatory displays. Audiovisual presentation. Gift shop.
Disabled access. Parking. £.
Open Easter-Oct: Apr, daily 14.00-17.00; May-Sep, daily
10.00-17.00; Oct, daily 14.00-17.00.
Tel: 01862 871351
Web: www.tarbat-discovery.co.uk

Teampull na Trionaid, Carinish
[Map: A5] Off A865, 4 miles NE of Balivanich, Carinish,
North Uist. (NGR: NF 816602 LR: 22)
Near the ruinous but interesting Church of The Trinity, or
Teampull na Trionaid in Gaelic, there was a holy well [NF
814601].

The church dates from the thirteenth or fourteenth century,
and was one of the largest pre-Reformation churches in the

Western Isles. It is believed to have been built around 1203 either by Beatrice, daughter of Somerled, or by Amy MacRuarie, first wife of John, Lord of the Isles.

The buildings are now ruinous, but the site was an important centre of learning in medieval times.

Parking nearby.

Access at all reasonable times.

Tigh an Tobar

[Map: F7] Off A9, 3 miles W of Blair Atholl, Tigh an Tobar, Perthshire. (NGR: NN 823654 LR: 43)

A spring here was used as a healing well.

The trees around the well were adorned with offerings of various kinds, and coins and buttons were thrown into the water. The well no longer appears to be regularly used but it was still being visited by many folk in the 1850s.

Tobar Bial na Buaidh, Dalvuie

[Map: D7] Off A828, 2 miles N of Connel, 1.5 miles SE of Benderloch, Dalvuie, Argyll. (NGR: NN 919370 LR: 49)

The healing well here was visited until at least the beginning of the nineteenth century. The name Tobar Bial na Buaidh means well of virtuous water in Gaelic.

Offerings were placed in a hollow in a nearby tree for the 'guardian spirit' of the water.

Tobar Chaluim Chille, Laiaval

[Map: A5] Off B893, 3.5 miles E of Sollas, Laiaval, North Uist. (NGR: NF 879750 LR: 18)

The well of St Columba or Tobar Chaluim Chille, is situated to the south-east of Laiaval, a low hill on the island of North Uist in the Western Isles.

The spring, forming a pool of water about ten feet across, is enclosed by low walling.

Tobar na Bile, Inverliever
[Map: D8] Off B840, 5 miles NE of Kilmartin, Inverliever,
Argyll. (NGR: NM 893056   LR: 55)
Tobar na Bile or well of (holy) trees, apparently predicted the
fortunes of the MacIvers of Inverliever: when the waters were
low some kind of trouble was at hand.

Barbreck's Bone, which is said to have cured madness and is
now in the Museum of Scotland, was said to have been found
in a nearby burial ground. It is a piece of elephant ivory, but
according to tradition it was said to be a magic bone which
had 'fallen from the heavens'.

Tobar na Suil, Luing
[Map: C8] Off unlisted road, 1.5 miles N of Toberonochy,
Luing. (NGR: NM 753114   LR: 55)
Water from this well on Luing was used to cure eye diseases:
the spring emerges into a small hollow, said to resemble an
eyeball (Suil is Gaelic for eye). The well is reported to have
been used at least as late as the 1970s – offerings were found
under an adjacent stone – and may still be in use today.

Tobar nam Buaidh, St Kilda
Gleann Mor, N side of St Kilda.
(NGR: NA 086002   LR: 18)
Tobar nam Buaidh, or well of virtue, was used to cure nervous
diseases, headaches and deafness. The spring is in a stone
wellhouse.

Tobar nan Dileag, Tullichuil
[Map: E7] Off A827, 2.5 miles E of Kenmore, Tullichuil,
Dull, Perthshire. (NGR: NN 805464   LR: 52)
Water from Tobar nan Dileag, or well of drips, was used in the
treatment of whooping cough. The spring drips from a rock
into a basin. It was still being visited by sick children at the
beginning of the twentieth century.

Trumpan Church
[Map: B5] Off B886, 8 miles NE of Dunvegan, Trumpan, Skye. (NGR: NG 225613 LR: 23)
The Truth Stone is located in the graveyard at Trumpan Church. The stone, which has a small hole near the top, was used as a form of trial or ordeal. The accused individual was blindfolded and they would then have to put their finger in the hole at the first attempt. This would prove that they were innocent of lying – but only if they succeeded the first time.

The ruins of a medieval church, previously with a thatched roof, was dedicated to St Conan and stand in an old burial ground. This was the scene of a cruel massacre when the congregation of MacLeods was burned to death in the church by party of raiding MacDonalds. The alarm was raised, and the MacLeods of Dunvegan, bringing with them the Fairy Flag, slaughtered the MacDonalds.
Parking Nearby.
Access at all reasonable times.

Up Helly Aa Exhibition, Lerwick
Off A970, St Sunniva Street, Lerwick, Shetland.
(NGR: HU 475415 LR: 4)
The exhibition is dedicated to the annual Shetland fire festival of Up Helly Aa. It features displays, artifacts, photographs, costumes and a replica ship.
Explanatory displays. Video. WC. Disabled access. Car and coach parking. £.
Open mid May-mid Sep, Tue 14.00-16.00 & 19.00-21.00, Fri 19.00-21.00, Sat 14.00-16.00.
Web: www.uphellyaa.org

Witch's Stone, Dornoch
[Map: E4] Off A949, Littledown, Dornoch, Sutherland.
(NGR: NH 797896 LR: 21)
The stone, a small upright slab inscribed with the date 1722, is said to mark the place where Janet Horne was executed.

She was reputedly the last witch to be burned in Scotland, although contemporary evidence is vague. Janet was accused of, among other things, turning her daughter into a pony, getting her shod, and riding her to meetings with the Devil. The daughter was reported to have been lame. One story has Horne been dragged through the streets of Dornoch, and then being burnt in a barrel of tar. The accusation appears to have been in 1727, rather than 1722 though. The stone stands in a private garden, but can be viewed.

Access at all reasonable times.

Witch's Stone, Spott

[Map: G9] Off A1 or B6370, 2.5 miles S of Dunbar, E side of Spott village, East Lothian. (NGR: NT 669752   LR: 67)

East Lothian has a rather dubious reputation for having had a large number of witch trials in the sixteenth and seventeenth centuries. Spott was one of the centres of accusations in 1662. The stone, which is enclosed by railings, is said to be near where Marion Lillie, the Ringwoodie Witch, was executed, reportedly in 1698. One story is that she was the last of those accused of witchcraft to be burnt in Scotland, but this is unlikely to be true as there are later stories from Dornoch and Crieff. Recent reports have coins, candle wax and the remains of incense being found at the stone.

There is now a plaque at the site.

Access at all reasonable times: park in village.

FURTHER READING

Beith, M. *Healing Threads*, Edinburgh, 1995.

Campbell, J. G. *Superstitions of the Highland and Islands of Scotland*, Glasgow, 1900.

Campbell, J. L. (editor) *A Collection of Highland Rites and Customs*, Cambridge, 1975.

Coventry, M. *Haunted Castles and Houses of Scotland*, Musselburgh, 2004.

Dalyell, J. *The Darker Superstitions of Scotland*, Edinburgh, 1835.

Davidson, T. *Rowan Tree and Red Thread*, Edinburgh, 1949.

Frazer, J. G *The Golden Bough: A Study in Magic and Religion*, London, 1922.

Goodare, J. (editor) *The Scottish Witch-hunt in Context*, Manchester, 2002.

Gordon, A. *Candie for the Foundling*, Edinburgh, 1992.

Henderson, L. and Cowan, E. J. *Scottish Fairy Belief*, East Linton, 2001.

Kirk, T *The Secret Common-Wealth*, 1691. Edited and commentary by S. Sanderson, Cambridge, 1976.

Larner, C *Enemies of God: The Witch-Hunt in Scotland*, Oxford, 1983.

Macdonald, S. *The Witches of Fife: Witch Hunting in a Scottish Shire, 1560-1710*, East Linton, 2002.

Mackinlay, J. M. *Folklore of Scottish Lochs and Springs*, Glasgow, 1893.

Maxwell-Stuart, P. G. *Satan's Conspiracy, Magic and Witchcraft in Sixteenth-century Scotland*, East Linton, 2001.

McLagan, R. C. *Evil Eye in the Western Highlands of Scotland*, London, 1902.

McNeill, F. M. *The Silver Bough*, (4 volumes), Glasgow, 1959.

McPherson, J. M. *Primitive Beliefs in the North East of Scotland*, London, 1929.

Martin, M. *A Description of the Western Islands of Scotland circa 1695*, Edinburgh, 1698, (facsimile edition, Edinburgh, 1994).

Sharpe, C. K. *A Historical Account of the Belief in Witchcraft in Scotland*, Glasgow, 1884.

Thomas, K. *Religion and the Decline of Magic*, London, 1971.

INDEX

157